GERMANY
BETWEEN TWO WARS

A Study of Propaganda and War-Guilt

Macnaghten

LINDLEY FRASER

OXFORD UNIVERSITY PRESS

LONDON   NEW YORK   TORONTO

1945

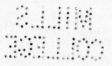

A WARTIME BOOK

THIS COMPLETE EDITION IS PRODUCED
IN FULL COMPLIANCE WITH THE GOVERN-
MENT'S REGULATIONS FOR CONSERVING
PAPER AND OTHER ESSENTIAL MATERIALS

PRINTED IN THE UNITED STATES OF AMERICA

PREFACE TO ENGLISH EDITION

THE writing of this book was undertaken in the spring of
1944 at the invitation of persons officially concerned with
the occupation and administration of Germany after the end of
the Second World War. It was primarily intended to be read
by Germans—as a means of showing them how they had been
misled by their own propagandists both before and during the
National Socialist régime. But it was also designed to assist
British and American officers and any others who may be in
contact with Germans in the immediate post-war years to understand the intellectual background of the people with whom they
will be dealing. It does not profess to be a *history* of the period
between the two wars. In the central chapters I have found it
convenient to adopt a narrative form of presentation, though
even there without any attempt to relate events in their chrono-
logical sequence. But essentially the book is an *argument*—a
reasoned refutation of the main articles of National Socialist
teachings on the origins of the war, and an exposition of the role
of propaganda as part of Hitler's preparations. Towards the
end of the book I attempt to show the extent to which Germany
as a whole can be considered guilty of the war—though without
entering into the unprofitable controversy as to whether there
are, or are not, 'good Germans'.

The English and American reader may feel that I have argued
certain points at unnecessary length, particularly in the last
section of Chapter I and in certain parts of Chapter VI, where
I deal with National Socialist allegations which seem to him too
obviously false—or too obviously unimportant—to deserve the
attention I have paid them. But all these allegations have been,
in their time, whole-heartedly and indeed passionately accepted
by many intelligent Germans—and the realization of that fact is
in itself a not unimportant contribution to our understanding
of the German mentality, which has shown itself amazingly able
to believe the incredible and attach weight to the trivial in all
questions relating to German national honour and German
national guiltlessness.

Much of the material of the book has been included in broadcasts delivered by me in German during my work as B.B.C.

German News Commentator. At the end of 1941 I delivered a series of talks which covered the main ground, and thereafter I and various of my colleagues from time to time reverted to the theme. We know that we were heard and that our arguments had some efficacy in shaking our listeners on the fundamental issue of war guilt—particularly when we dealt with the theme of the secret rearmament of Germany during the twenties and early thirties (see Chapter IV of the present work). But the material used in these broadcasts has been greatly added to and revised, the argument elaborated, the subject-matter rearranged, and the whole case against the National Socialist version of the events of the last thirty years presented from a post-war point of view. The book must not be thought of as simply a reprint of a series of broadcast talks.

I have made no attempt to provide an exhaustive list of my sources and authorities. References on particular points have, however, been included in footnotes to the text. And more generally I must acknowledge my debt to Mr. Gathorne Hardy's *Survey of International Affairs*, and to the following Oxford Pamphlets: Falls, *Was Germany defeated in 1918?*; Arnold Foster, *The Blockade of Germany, 1914–19*; Wheeler-Bennett, *The Treaties of Brest-Litovsk*; Gathorne Hardy, *The Fourteen Points and the Treaty of Versailles*; R. R. Kuczynski, *Living Space and Population Problems*; and Brierly, *Encirclement*.

I could not have written this book in the middle of my other labours had I not had the assistance and advice of a number of my colleagues and friends, to all of whom—and particularly to Mr. Duncan Wilson, Dr. H. Koeppler, Mr. S. D. Stirk, and Miss A. Andrews—my best thanks are due. The British Broadcasting Corporation generously allowed me a month's special leave in March 1944, during which I was able to write the first draft of the manuscript.

LINDLEY FRASER

B.B.C., BUSH HOUSE

LONDON

3 September, 1944

CONTENTS

FALSIS OPINIONIBVS REJECTIS
DEBELLATIS OPPRESSORIBVS
RATIONIS ITERVM SPES

INTRODUCTION

LONG before the outbreak of war, it was a commonplace that the National Socialist propaganda machine did not believe in truth. Every non-German was aware of this, many people were at least half aware of it inside Germany itself. But it nevertheless succeeded in imposing its interpretation of current history upon the great mass of the German people. By methods vividly described in Hitler's *Mein Kampf* it succeeded in evoking in many Germans' minds a series of simple, and largely false, propositions as to the course of world events from the middle of the First World War to the outbreak of the Second. By constant repetition in speeches, in newspaper articles, in wireless talks, in private conversations, and above all in the schoolroom, those concerned—and they were not only to be found in the ranks of the National Socialist Party—succeeded in bemusing the great mass of their fellow-countrymen, and some people in other countries, into believing these propositions. By so doing they prepared the German people for the part they required it to play in their schemes for aggression and conquest—the part of providing the necessary cannon-fodder for the Second World War.

These propositions, which together constitute what I may call the National Socialist version of the origins of the Second World War, can be set out as follows:

(1) 'The German army was in the military sense never beaten in 1918 but was stabbed in the back.'

(2) 'Germany was induced to lay down her arms in 1918 by the promise of a peace based on President Wilson's Fourteen Points. This promise was cynically broken by the Allies in the Treaty of Versailles which utterly ignored the principles which the American President had enunciated.'

(3) 'After the armistice the Allies deliberately maintained the naval blockade, refused to allow foodstuffs to be imported into Germany, and thus were wantonly responsible for untold misery and suffering to German civilians, and particularly to children, after the war was supposedly over.'

(4) 'By their harsh economic measures against Germany, and particularly by their extortionate demands for reparations, as well as by depriving Germany of vital economic resources in

Europe and of her colonies overseas, the Allies were directly responsible for the inflation of the early twenties and for the depression of the early thirties.'

(5) 'As soon as Hitler came to power he worked for peace and prosperity and international co-operation. The other Great Powers in Europe set themselves out to thwart him. They rejected his offers of friendship, they obstructed his efforts to reinstate Germany in her rightful place, they carried out a policy of encirclement and economic strangulation.' And therefore:

(6) 'The Second World War was engineered by Germany's enemies, was forced upon Germany, was from the German point of view a just war and a war of self-defence.'

These six propositions constitute the version of the origins of the Second World War which has been hammered into the minds of the German people for the last eleven years and more. Let us see how far they correspond with the facts.

THE END OF THE FIRST WORLD WAR

1.

WAS Germany defeated in the First World War? To the outside world the question seemed highly academic. The German Government, at the direct request of the High Command, had sued for an armistice; the German Army had laid down its arms; the Imperial Government which had been responsible for conducting the war vanished and in its place there was set up a new Government whose unenviable task it was to negotiate peace and accept the consequences of a lost war. If this is not defeat, the ordinary Englishman or American will say to himself, then words have lost their meaning. And because it seemed so obvious to him that Germany had been defeated by the end of 1918, he never took seriously the controversy which grew up inside Germany on precisely this point.

In this attitude the Western Powers made a grave mistake; they showed a complete failure to understand the German attitude. If they had taken the trouble to find out *why* as early as 1919 or 1920 the view was spreading among wide sections of the German people that Germany was *not* defeated in the First World War, they might have grasped at a much earlier moment the real significance of the rise of National Socialism; and perhaps the Second World War might have been prevented.

But before we come on to this question let us summarize the military facts of the situation.

For this purpose it is not necessary to go back earlier than the beginning of 1918. Germany entered the last year of the First World War with justifiably bright hopes of carrying it through to an early favourable conclusion. True, Hindenburg had been disappointed in the weapon on which he had set the greatest store in the previous year. The introduction of unrestricted U-boat warfare had not brought England to her knees; and, on the other hand, it was directly responsible for the entry of the United States into the war on the side of the Allies. But that was not necessarily disastrous for Germany's hopes. Hindenburg had understood all along that America was not likely to remain neutral when U-boats were sinking American merchant ships. But he reckoned that it would take the United States many months to mobilize its huge war potential and in the meantime he hoped to be able to administer the final blow to Germany's European enemies.

By the beginning of 1918 this hope seemed fully justified. Italy had been defeated. Russia had collapsed. Rumania was on the point of collapse. With the elimination of the enemy on the east, he was able to transfer more than forty trained divisions to the western front; with the result that in the spring of 1918 the German armies in the west, for the first time since the beginning of the war, were numerically substantially superior to their opponents. Nor was that all. The defeat of Italy and Rumania meant that no immediate danger threatened Germany from the south. The southern fronts could therefore safely be entrusted to Germany's two allies, Austria and Bulgaria. All they had to do was to hold on and guard Germany's flank while Germany herself administered the decisive blow against the tired and disheartened French and British armies on the west.

But the decisive blow had to be dealt quickly, before America could deploy her full strength. And when Hindenburg went over to the offensive in March 1918 it was with the intention, and in the confident expectation, of knocking the Allies out by the summer.

That he came almost within sight of achieving his goal is not to be questioned. The offensive down the Somme brought the Paris–Amiens railway under fire and threatened to sever the vital link between the main French army and the British positions in Flanders. The offensive up the valley of the Lys in the north dislocated the communications of the British armies. To the south the German armies advanced to Château-Thierry and cut the main line from Paris eastwards. By these three offensives Hindenburg almost succeeded in splitting the Allied armies into four separate and disorganized groups.

And yet the spring offensive failed. Why it failed we need not discuss. It may be that the Germans for all their numerical strength were not sufficiently superior in numbers and gun-fire to drive their attack home. Or it may be that Ludendorff's strategy was not the equal of his tactics and that he failed to exploit his successes to the best advantage.[1] The vital point is that

[1] The Military Correspondent of the London *Times*, Captain Cyril Falls, argues that the big mistake made by the German High Command was in

by the middle of July the force of the German blows was already weakening and the Allies were not knocked out. They had taken heavy punishment, had suffered serious losses in men, material, and territory, but they still had something in hand. On July 18 Foch launched the first counter-offensive—against the flank of the most southerly of the three German salients, that on the Aisne–Marne sector. It was completely successful in its object. Ludendorff was forced to retire from Château-Thierry back to the Aisne, the railway line from Paris eastwards was freed, and in addition the French took 30,000 German prisoners.

Then came the second and much more important Allied counter-offensive. On August 8 (the 'black day of the German Army', as Ludendorff called it[1]) the British armies attacked south-east of Amiens and broke through the German front-line positions. A fortnight later they attacked in even greater force north-east of Amiens and in four days had reached the key town of Bapaume. At the same time the French attacked farther south, between the Oise and Soissons, while five days later the British launched yet another offensive to the north, in the neighbourhood of Arras. By the beginning of September the German Army was in full, if orderly, retreat; but in these seven weeks it had lost 130,000 men as prisoners (to say nothing of tens of thousands killed and wounded) and a corresponding quantity of guns and equipment.

All these were simply counter-offensives. They were carried out by the Allies with strictly limited objectives in mind— namely to free their own communications and to remove the German threat to such key centres as Hazebrouck and Amiens. But they had the double effect of completely destroying the German spring offensive and of transferring the initiative into Allied hands, where it remained for the remainder of the war. Now came the crucial moment: the moment at which the Allies passed over from counter-offensive to offensive proper. At the end of September a series of assaults were launched on all parts of the front, from Flanders in the north to Argonne in the south-east. The main purpose was nothing less than to destroy the

pushing south to the Marne after the unexpectedly easy success of the Aisne offensive, instead of transferring the artillery used in that offensive to the north for a further assault upon the British positions in Flanders.

[1] *Kriegserinnerungen*, p. 547.

whole basis of the German Army's supplies by cutting the vital railway lines which ran from the war zone to Germany on either side of the Ardennes—namely the lines running up through the bottle-neck of Liége and the line running south-east towards Luxembourg. The German armies in the whole of the western front, from the Channel down to Rheims almost due east of Paris, depended exclusively on these two lines for reinforcements and supplies. These two lines were also the only routes along which a retreat back into Germany could be staged. If they were cut, then the whole German Army would have been rounded up and forced to surrender.

That was the position when in November Germany sued for an armistice. During the preceding three months the German armies on the west had lost more than a quarter of their total strength by capture, and getting on for another quarter in casualties; they had also been deprived of at least a half of their guns. Thus weakened on the main battle front they were faced with new responsibilities on the south; for in the middle of September Austria, already on the verge of collapse, made proposals to the Allies for a separate peace and two weeks later Bulgaria surrendered. The way was thus open for an Allied advance through the Balkans—which could only be stopped, if at all, by the transfer of large German forces from the west. By the beginning of November both Turkey and Austria had concluded armistices and Germany stood alone. Meanwhile American troops, fresh and well equipped, were pouring across the Atlantic in hundreds of thousands and the Allies were preparing their plans for a great offensive in the spring of 1919, accompanied by large-scale air raids on Germany itself.[1]

2.

So much for the purely military side of the story. Now let us turn to the political side—the relations between the High Command and the Civilian Government at home. After August 8, the black day, Hindenburg and Ludendorff became increasingly aware of the seriousness of the situation. They recognized the gravity of the threats from the west, they knew that Austria and Bulgaria were no longer to be relied on, and they also were

[1] By the end of the war the Allies had achieved a decisive qualitative and quantitative air superiority over Germany. See on this (for example) Fokker's *Autobiography*.

coming to have doubts about the fighting spirit of the German Army itself—a point to which we shall return later on. On August 14 a Crown Council was held at which the situation was discussed; and at this council Ludendorff declared his conviction that the war could no longer be won in the field. Crown Prince Rupprecht of Bavaria, one of the three Army Group Commanders, shared this view. On August 15 he wrote: 'I no longer believe that we can hold out over the winter; it is even possible that a catastrophe will occur earlier. . . . What we must do if we are to avoid a military disaster . . . is to make haste to approach our enemies . . . with peace offers.'[1] Nothing came of these suggestions; they were advocated by the soldiers, but the Civilian Government was reluctant to embark upon them. Six weeks later the matter came to a crisis. On September 29 Ludendorff and Hindenburg went directly to the Kaiser and demanded that a telegram be sent forthwith to the American President with proposals for peace and a request for an immediate armistice. On the same day the internal situation in Germany was drastically altered by the sudden granting by the Kaiser of new and extensive powers of participation by the Reichstag in the activities of the Civilian Government. The Chancellor, Hertling, offered his resignation which was accepted by the Kaiser. His successor was Prince Max of Baden. The latter fought against Ludendorff's view. First he refused to consider the proposal to appeal to the American President at all. Then he urged that only a peace offer should be made, without the request for an armistice. But Ludendorff insisted; 'I want to save my army', he said; and four days later, on October 3, Hindenburg wrote to the Reich Chancellor in the following terms:

'The Supreme Command continues to hold to its demand . . . that a request for an armistice should be sent to our enemies immediately. As a result of the collapse on the Macedonian front . . . and the impossibility of making good the very severe losses we have suffered . . . on the western front there is, so far as it is humanly possible to judge, no further chance of forcing a peace on the enemy. . . . The German Army still stands firm. . . . Nevertheless . . . the circumstances call for a cessation of hostilities.'[2]

On receipt of this letter, which could hardly have been

---

[1] *The Memoirs of Prince Max of Baden* (English edition), vol. i, p. 320.
[2] *Amtliche Urkunden*, No. 33.

couched in stronger terms, Prince Max yielded and that night
sent off the telegram to President Wilson in the terms demanded.

Now comes an extremely tortuous and intricate series of
developments. President Wilson answered the German Reich
Chancellor's message on October 9. He demanded to know
whether Germany, in the event of an armistice, would at once
withdraw her armies within the boundaries of the Reich. Prince
Max asked Ludendorff whether Germany could safely refuse
this condition. Ludendorff refused to give a straight answer.
Without committing himself, he implied that he was not now
so anxious for an armistice as he had been ten days previously.

Three days later, on October 13, the Civilian Government
took matters into their own hands. They announced to the
Government of the United States that they agreed to evacuate
all invaded territories and they also stated that they now
accepted President Wilson's Fourteen Points as a basis for peace.
On the 16th came the American reply. It stated that the conditions of the armistice must be left to the judgement of the
Allied military advisers; in other words, it specifically refused to
concede the Fourteen Points as a basis for negotiating the laying
down of German arms.[1] Next day Prince Max again saw
Ludendorff. Again Ludendorff was evasive; behind a torrent
of words and arguments about a soldier's luck, a further comb-
out of German industry, insufficient food-supplies for the
German troops, declining morale and the like, he contrived to
give no positive guidance to the War Cabinet. Again the
Civilian Government was forced to take matters into its own
hands. It decided that the negotiations for peace must continue; and it also decided that Ludendorff must be removed.
On October 26 Ludendorff resigned. One of his last acts had
been to persuade Hindenburg to issue (on October 24) a proclamation to the German Army calling upon it to continue the
struggle.

Ludendorff's successor was General Gröner. When he was
asked by the Chancellor how long the German Army could hold
out while armistice negotiations were in progress, his answer
was that that depended on how long the German Army could
prevent the Allies from cutting the vital railway line from
Luxembourg. In the early days of November the American

---

[1] On the attitude of the Allies at this time to the Fourteen Points as a
basis for *peace* (as opposed to an armistice) see Chapter III below.

advance on Mezières came to represent a major and urgent
threat; on the 6th Gröner told Prince Max that the railway
could not be held and that if an armistice was not concluded
within a week 'the white flag will have to cross the line'. On
hearing this the Chancellor dispatched a delegation to Marshal
Foch, with powers to negotiate an armistice on whatever terms
the Allies could be persuaded to accept.

In all this complicated story, there is one question which
cries out for an answer. Up to the beginning of October, as we
have seen, the High Command, that is to say Hindenburg and
Ludendorff, took a more pessimistic view than the Civilian
Government and were responsible for forcing an unwilling
Chancellor to open negotiations with President Wilson. By the
middle of October, on the other hand, it was the Civilian
Government which was forcing the pace, whereas Hindenburg
and Ludendorff were expressing vague hopes of being able to
hold out. What is the explanation of this reversal of roles?
As regards the Government there is no difficulty. Its members
did not understand the seriousness of the military situation
until, at the end of September, they allowed themselves to be
reluctantly convinced by the insistent demands for armistice
negotiations on the part of the High Command. But once the
true situation had been borne in upon them, they drew the
necessary conclusions and acted upon them. Moreover, the
Government in Berlin was well aware that during the month of
October pessimism, discouragement, and distrust of the Imperial
regime had been growing among the civilian population at home.
By the beginning of November it realized that a cessation of
hostilities could not be postponed without imminent danger of
complete disaster—the more so as the refusal of the sailors of
the High Sea Fleet to sail out to challenge the British Navy had
shown that even members of the German armed forces were
no longer prepared to throw away their lives in a gesture of
empty bravado. All this is clear and straightforward.
But what of the attitude of the High Command? How did
it come about that Hindenburg and Ludendorff, who had
demanded immediate armistice negotiations at the end of
September, appeared to be disposed to continue the struggle
two weeks later?
Had something happened in between to make the situation

look less hopeless than at the beginning of the month? The
course of events as described above refutes that possibility. If
the military situation was black by the end of September, it was
even blacker by the middle of October, with the successful
launching of the general Allied offensive and the imminent
collapse of the southern front.

Or had the High Command ground for thinking that its
earlier judgement was too pessimistic? Again the answer must
be a decisive negative. The High Command had not exaggerated the threat to the German armies from west and south
when it advised the Government on October 3 that there was
'no further chance of forcing a peace on the enemy'.

No, Ludendorff's and Hindenburg's change of standpoint
cannot be accounted for in terms of improved military prospects
or the discovery that an earlier appraisement of the situation
was mistaken. The explanation is more complicated than that.

In the first place Ludendorff himself had gone through a
nervous crisis at the end of September. By October he had
temporarily recovered and was perhaps genuinely inclined to
take an over-optimistic view of the situation.

Secondly, it is possible that the German High Command was
unduly optimistic about the exhaustion and war-weariness of
the Allies.

Thirdly, by the middle of October it was becoming clear to
the German authorities that the Allies were not likely to conclude peace so long as the Kaiser remained head of the German
State. It may have been that this knowledge stiffened him in
his decision to oppose the armistice negotiations.

But behind Ludendorff's changed attitude lay a further factor
of a very different type. Ludendorff himself gives us the clue
to it. In a memorandum written on October 31—five days after
his dismissal—he wrote regarding the events that led up to that
dismissal:

'Our situation could certainly not have been improved. Events in
the south-east were bound to take their course—of that there could
be no doubt. But a tremendous effort on the part of the German
nation would have had a sobering effect on the peoples and armies
of France and England, and probably also of America. We could
have held out for a few more months. The garrison of a fortress
which capitulates before it is utterly exhausted lies under the stigma
of dishonour.'[1]

[1] See the official report of the German Parliamentary Commission of

This statement is important and revealing in a number of different ways. In the first place Ludendorff makes it perfectly clear that he still believed, as a month earlier, that the German Army had no further hope of victory. No suggestion that he—or Hindenburg—believed defeat to be avoidable can be entertained for a moment.

But Ludendorff did think, or said he thought, that by fighting on for a short time the German Army might gain better terms for Germany than if it capitulated at once. And he also professed to have realized that to sue for an armistice before one is finally exhausted is dishonourable. Now this last point, if he were sincere about it at all, cannot have been absent from his mind when he and Hindenburg demanded the opening of armistice negotiations a month previously. It cannot be wholly honourable to lay down arms in September but dishonourable to lay them down in October, especially if the military situation has deteriorated still further in the meantime!

Therefore, on one or other of the two occasions—or on both—Ludendorff was being dishonest. Either he and Hindenburg did not really want an armistice at the beginning of October; or, secondly, he did not at the end of October really think an armistice dishonourable; or, thirdly—since these two alternatives do not exclude one another—he *neither* wanted an armistice *nor* thought an armistice dishonourable.

I have no doubt that the last possibility gives the true answer to the position taken up by Ludendorff and Hindenburg during that fateful month of October 1918. In other words, I believe that the demand for an armistice at the end of September was to some extent at least a piece of strategic deception practised, not merely against the Allies, but also against the German Government and the German people. And I also believe that the memorandum of October 31 was equally a piece of deception, though of a very different and even more fateful kind.

What Hindenburg and Ludendorff wanted at the end of September was above all things *time*. They were more interested in armistice negotiations than in an actual armistice; and much more interested in an armistice than in the conclusion of peace. Their view was that however hopeless her military situation, from a medium or long-term point of view, Germany still had

Inquiry entitled *Die Ursachen des Zusammenbruches im Jahre 1918*, vol. ii, p. 367.

a potent short-term bargaining counter; namely, the fact that she *could* go on fighting if necessary for a further few months. This bargaining weapon must be preserved if at all possible, not merely during the armistice negotiations, but also during the peace negotiations which would follow. Only so, they argued, could Germany hope to obtain relatively favourable peace terms.

In fact this plan did not succeed, owing to President Wilson's cold response to the German overtures. But it is worth while to consider briefly what was hoped from it. Suppose that the Allies had agreed to an armistice on the terms Ludendorff and Hindenburg wanted; terms, namely, which left the German Army intact and fully armed in possession of at least a part of Belgium and northern France, pending a final settlement. The Allied advance would then have been stopped while peace negotiations were in progress, and in the meantime Germany would be given a breathing-space. This she would have used to good purpose. There would have been time to carry through the further comb-out of industry about which Ludendorff spoke to the War Cabinet on October 17. New defensive positions could be prepared along a suitable line, perhaps far to the rear, perhaps on, or inside, the frontiers of the Reich itself; divisions could be re-formed, battle-weary units replaced by fresh ones; above all, the High Command would have uninterrupted use of the two vital railway routes on either side of the Ardennes, which they could use either for bringing up supplies to the front, or else (if a general retreat were decided upon) for withdrawing the main armies back to Aachen and the Moselle or even to the east bank of the Rhine. Germany would then be in a far better position, as a result of the breathing-space, to bargain with the Allies on the terms of the peace. For if the terms demanded by the Allies were too harsh, Germany could threaten to break off the negotiations; and the Allies would then be faced with having to take up the struggle under less favourable conditions than at the beginning of the breathing-space, and knowing that though the final result was still not in doubt, yet its achievement would be costly and painful.

Moreover, this line of thought was linked up with another, even more tortuous one. The High Command was aware that in democratic countries the actions of governments are influenced by the knowledge of what the people as a whole thinks and wants. Might they not turn this fact to their own advantage?

Suppose they invited and entered into armistice negotiations and this fact became generally known in England, France, and America, the popular reaction would be one of overwhelming relief and joy that the end of the war was in sight.[1] Still more if an armistice were actually concluded and the belligerents got round the conference table to discuss terms of peace; in that case even if the Allied Governments were prepared to resume hostilities rather than concede lenient terms, yet they might perhaps be overruled by pressure from public opinion in their own countries. By this means too—by, so to speak, working on the peoples of the democratic countries over the heads of their governments—Germany might obtain more favourable treatment than she could hope for on the basis of military considerations taken by themselves.

I have no doubt that reasons of this sort played a considerable part in determining the policy of the High Command during the last two months of the war. In support of this view, I recall Ludendorff's own words, cited above: 'A tremendous effort on the part of the German nation would have had a *sobering effect* on the *peoples and armies*' of the Allies. It is worth while also quoting what Max of Baden wrote later about the attitude of Germany's then rulers to peace negotiations as an instrument of national policy. 'The Supreme Command probably saw in Wilson's Fourteen Points a mere collection of phrases, which a skilful diplomacy would be able to interpret at the conference table in a sense favourable to Germany.'[2]

Precisely this attitude had manifested itself nearly two years earlier, at the time of the famous 'peace offer' from the Central Powers to the Allies, to which we shall come back later. That peace offer was not meant genuinely: the language in which it was couched was enough to show this by itself. Its purpose was, among other things, to split and weaken public opinion in the western democracies. Some people in France and England might be inclined to take it seriously, others would reject it; all would, however, be buoyed up to a state of false optimism by it and the long-term result would be—so the German rulers

---

[1] In actual fact, when the Germans applied for an armistice the news came as a surprise, not merely to public opinion in the Allied countries, but also, as Mr. Churchill recalled a year or two ago, to the Allied Governments, who had, at the time, no doubt that the war would continue into the spring of 1919.

[2] *The Memoirs of Prince Max of Baden*, vol. ii, p. 24.

reckoned—a weakening in the unity and fighting spirit of Germany's main enemies.[1]

But the desire to achieve a diplomatic success and to 'carry the war on by other means' was not the only thing that Ludendorff had in mind when he and Hindenburg pursued their tortuous course during the six weeks before the armistice. They had another, even more important purpose in view; namely to place the responsibility for the admission of Germany's defeat on the shoulders of the Reich Government rather than accepting it themselves.

In achieving this object the first task was to implant firmly in the mind of the Government the knowledge that the war was already lost. The ground for this was prepared during August in the interview between Hindenburg and the then Chancellor, Hertling (along with Hintze, the Foreign Secretary), and again in Ludendorff's statement to the Crown Council on the same day (August 14). When the Government proved unexpectedly obstinate, shock tactics were employed—namely the direct approach to the Kaiser on September 29. During the next few days the heat was applied remorselessly, until (as we have seen) the new Chancellor, Max of Baden, at last gave way. It was he, not Hindenburg, who signed the message to President Wilson on October 3. And from that day onwards, all negotiations, or proposals for negotiations, came ostensibly from the civilian authorities. Even the armistice delegation which interviewed Foch at Compiègne was a governmental delegation. The Army was represented only by a liaison officer, General von Winterfeldt. So the High Command was in a position to say afterwards that *it* had had no part in the negotiations for ending hostilities.

But it was not enough for the High Command simply to sit back and dissociate itself from the negotiations it had itself precipitated. In order firmly to establish its claim that the *Army's* honour (as opposed to the German people's) had been unsmirched, Ludendorff and Hindenburg had to put up a show of actively *opposing* the negotiations. And that is what they did —Ludendorff in his interview with Prince Max on October 10 and in his session with the War Cabinet a week later; Hindenburg in his proclamation to the Army on October 24. It will be noted that in none of their utterances at the time did either of

[1] For the text of this offer and the other reasons which inspired it see below, Chapter VI.

them advise explicitly *against* proceeding with armistice negotiations. That they could not risk doing, lest they be taken at their word and the armistice negotiations called off. But they manœuvred themselves into a position in which they, the soldiers, were apparently advocating—unsuccessfully—a continuation of the war in the face of demands for peace from a group of irreconcilably defeatist civilians.

It was cleverly done, and it paved the way for the future story that in the First World War the German Army remained unbeaten to the end. Yet behind the scenes a different picture was being painted. On November 6, as we have seen, General Gröner told Prince Max that the surrender of the Army was now only a matter of days. And when the leader of the armistice delegation, Erzberger, saw Hindenburg before setting out for Compiègne, the Commander-in-Chief told him that for the sake of the Army he must accept any conditions the Allies chose to impose. By that time, in fact, the military situation was not merely hopeless from a long-term point of view—it had been that at least since the end of September—it was then and there desperate. The Government had to hurry to carry through the negotiations; otherwise the Army might have had to surrender. And Prince Max of Baden, writing about this period in his memoirs, showed that he too shared and accepted the Hindenburg–Ludendorff point of view on this matter. 'Our prevailing feeling', he says, 'was one of relief that at least the *Army* would not have to wait on Foch.'[1] That was after he knew that the Allies were prepared to conduct negotiations with the Government. Foch himself, it is known, was opposed to this concession. He wanted to receive the surrender of the German Army, and it is clear from the evidence I have just given that he would not have had to wait long before getting it. But he was overborne by the Governments of the Western Powers; with the result that part at least of Ludendorff's plan succeeded. He had not achieved his first goal of using Germany's capacity to fight on as a bargaining weapon for enforcing milder armistice terms. But he had 'saved his army'—from the humiliation of a formal capitulation. And with this he had opened the doors to the doctrine of the 'stab-in-the-back'.

[1] *The Memoirs of Prince Max of Baden*, vol. ii, p. 305.

3.

The origin and rise to power of the stab-in-the-back theory is interesting and instructive. Shortly after the conclusion of the armistice, a British general, Sir Neill Malcolm, was dining with Ludendorff in Berlin. The subject came round to the reasons for Germany's collapse. Ludendorff naturally, and entirely understandably, sought for explanations which would exculpate himself and his strategy and would not reflect on the reputation of the German Army. And he found them in long complaints, embodied in that turgid and involved eloquence of which he was a master, against the Reich Government and the civilian population, which, he alleged, had failed to support him, had let him down, had proved itself unworthy of the traditions of a fighting nation. General Malcolm sought to crystallize Ludendorff's meaning in a sentence: 'You mean, General Ludendorff,' he inquired sceptically, 'that you were—were *stabbed in the back*?' Ludendorff's eye lit up in fierce enthusiasm as he heard the phrase. 'That's it exactly,' he shouted; 'we were *stabbed in the back*—STABBED IN THE BACK!' And during the next few months Ludendorff saw to it that the idea, and even the phrase 'stab-in-the-back', was firmly implanted in the minds of his friends and colleagues. He was so successful that when, some months later, in November 1919, Hindenburg came to give evidence in the Reichstag building before the Commission of Inquiry into the conduct of the war, he summarized his evidence in the following words:

'Our repeated request for the maintenance of stern discipline and the strict application of the law, met with no results. Our operations in consequence failed, as they were bound to, and the collapse became inevitable. The Revolution was merely the last straw. *As an English General has very truly said: the German Army was stabbed in the back.*'[1]

[1] Wheeler-Bennett, *Hindenburg, the Wooden Titan*, p. 238 (my italics). At the time it was widely supposed that the English General to whom Hindenburg referred was Sir Frederick Maurice, who was alleged to have given support to the stab-in-the-back theory in his book *The Last Four Months of the War*. But that book contains nothing remotely resembling any such theory and in due course Sir Frederick Maurice issued a formal *démenti* to the German Press, in the course of which he stated categorically 'there is no doubt that the German armies were thoroughly and decisively beaten in the field'. This *démenti* was soon forgotten. There seems no doubt that the association of the theory with 'an English General' really derives from

So the stab-in-the-back theory was launched on the world, with the official blessing of the German Commander-in-Chief. That it was fathered on to a British general was an additional support to it, since many Germans, who might have remained sceptical if it had appeared solely under Hindenburg's or Ludendorff's name, were convinced of its truth when they believed it came from one of Germany's opponents in the field. But even if the true story of its origin, as described above, had been published in Germany, it would not have made any difference in the long run to its currency. For it was a story that many people wanted for their own ends to tell and still more were glad to believe. To many patriotic Germans, smarting under the humiliation of their country's failure in war, it gave the reassurance that at least the German Army had preserved its honour and its claim to invincibility. To the military leaders it offered a welcome answer to any suggestion that the unfavourable end to the war was due to their mistakes in strategy. For the officers and professional soldiers it was a means of maintaining self-respect, and confidence for the future. And finally, for the propagandists and the National Socialists, it was a God-given weapon for maintaining and reviving the belief in Germans as a fighting race and in war as a legitimate, creditable, and potent way of furthering national policy. The theory was taken up and developed by countless writers, not by any means all of them of nationalist or imperialist views.[1] Only a few years after the conclusion of peace, the great majority of Germans probably regarded the theory as an unquestioned and universally accepted truth.

There were, however, exceptions; Germans who regarded the theory as being not merely contrary to the facts but as constituting an unwarranted slander on the German people. And their point of view came out into the open seven years after the end of the war, in October 1925. The occasion was a lawsuit, in which the main contestants were two Munich editors. Professor Cossmann had for some time devoted much space in his periodical the *Süddeutsche Monatshefte* to expounding and

the dinner-table conversation between Ludendorff and General Malcolm, as described above.
[1] One of the most explicit versions of the theory known to me was that published by a Liberal, Dr. Edgar Stern Rubarth, then editor of the Wolff Telegraph Agency, in his book *Die Propaganda als Politisches Instrument*. See in particular Preface and pp. 22, 62.

developing the stab-in-the-back theory. The issue was taken up in the social-democratic *Münchener Post*, where Cossmann was accused of falsifying historical fact and poisoning political life. So Cossmann brought an action for slander against Guber, the editor of the *Münchener Post*. Many witnesses were called on both sides and of course the main subject at issue was the question of fact: was it or was it not true as a pure matter of history that the German Army had been stabbed in the back? Among those who denied the truth of the theory were two whose testimony is worth quoting from. The first is General Kuhl, who had been Chief of Staff to Rupert of Bavaria. His attitude is the more interesting in that he was called on behalf of the prosecution—i.e. of Cossmann and the stab-in-the-back theory. Among other things he said: 'We could have carried on the war longer . . . admittedly not to victory, final victory was no longer possible. . . . I am convinced that the war was lost with the failure of the spring offensive.' And General Kuhl went on, 'In my view it is not correct to use the phrase "stab in the back" in its usual sense, as though the Army were victorious but was attacked in the rear from home and as though that were the only cause of our losing the war.'[1]

The second witness to be quoted here is Dr. Eugen Fischer, a former army officer who had been secretary to the Parliamentary Commission of Inquiry at which Hindenburg first formally enunciated the stab-in-the-back theory. Dr. Fischer went even farther than General Kuhl. He said:

'I flatly deny that there was any stab in the back. I am convinced that the idea arose because of the need of the Right Wing Parties to find a scapegoat. . . . They wished to build up the past again, and called out for a scapegoat so as to rescue the authorities of the past from dishonour—and their cry found its expression in the legend, the slogan, the illusion of a stab in the back.'[2]

But these voices were in a minority. Cossmann won his case against Guber and the result of the trial was doubtless merely to strengthen the conviction in the minds of the great majority of Germans that the stab-in-the-back version of the end of the First World War was an established fact. When the National Socialists came into power eight years later, they found the soil well prepared for the planting of their own special corollary to

[1] *Der Dolchstoss Prozess, Eine Ehrenrettung des Deutschen Volkes*, Oct.-Nov. 1925, pp. 90-2.
[2] Ibid., p. 355.

the doctrine: 'next time it will be different; next time there will be victory'.

4.

That is the story of the rise of the stab-in-the-back theory. What of its validity? One might have supposed that the facts set out in the preceding pages would have been enough to dispose of it. But many Germans to whom those facts were well known have passionately supported the theory. On what grounds do they base their case?

Three questions or groups of questions must be distinguished here. First, was the German Army defeated in the First World War, and if so in what sense was it defeated? Secondly, if the German Army *was* defeated, to what causes can that defeat be attributed? And thirdly, if those causes had not been present, or could have been removed, what would the effect have been on the outcome of the war? Let us take these questions in turn.

The question whether the German Army was or was not defeated is, in the light of the historical events set out in the first pages of this chapter, essentially a matter of the use of words. It was not defeated *if* by 'defeated' one means totally destroyed or dissolved. Many writers have pointed, with not illegitimate pride, to the fact that throughout the great retreats of the summer and autumn it remained intact and an 'army'.

Nor, secondly, did it ever finally surrender to its opponents in the field. As we have seen, it was the Reich Government, under its Chancellor, Prince Max of Baden, which took upon itself the onus, and the odium, of having negotiated the actual cessation of hostilities.

On the other hand, the German Army clearly *was* beaten in innumerable engagements and battles, it had wholly lost the initiative, was in headlong retreat, had in three months sacrificed half of its man-power and artillery, had no more reserves, was faced with an ever-growing numerical, material, and technical superiority on the side of its opponents.

Not merely that, but by the beginning of November it was admitted—by Gröner to the Chancellor, by Hindenburg to Erzberger[1]—that unless hostilities ceased at once, on whatever terms, the Army could not escape the final step of wholesale surrender. As we have seen, the armistice came just in time to

[1] See above, p. 15.

save it from that fate. Furthermore, though it still retained a framework of order and discipline, yet discontent, insubordination, and desertions were becoming ever more common. We shall come back in a moment to the significance of this phenomenon and to the use made of it by exponents of the stab-in-the-back theory. For the moment what matters is the *fact*. As early as August, Ludendorff was told, according to his own account, how 'troops falling back cried out to a fresh division marching bravely to the attack "Strike breakers" '.[1] By the beginning of October he was telling the Government: 'The troops are holding out to-day—but nobody knows what may happen to-morrow.'[2] There can be no doubt, in short, that by November the complete collapse of the German Army was imminent.

Under these circumstances, to say that the German Army emerged unbeaten in the field from the First World War is simply to play with words. Think of a boxer at the end of a long and gruelling fight. In the last few rounds he has taken severe punishment and is clearly nearing the end of his strength. He has not yet been given the knock-out blow, nor has he collapsed on to the floor of the ring from his own weakness; but one or other of these alternatives is clearly inevitable and his seconds decide that it is no use prolonging the agony and throw in the towel. That boxer has been *beaten*, has lost the match against his opponent; and though his supporters may offer explanations and excuses for his failure, yet no one in his senses will try to argue that he did *not* fail!

At the risk of being tedious, let me approach the point from another angle. What do we mean by the word 'army'? It is a body of men intended for fighting and duly trained, equipped, organized, and disciplined so as to fight efficiently. As such it is not something separate from, or over and above, the human beings (and equipment) of which it is composed; it is simply these human beings arranged, and behaving, in a particular way. It follows that if these human beings cease to be good at their jobs—if the commander makes mistakes in strategy or tactics, if the officers fail to give the right orders to their troops, if the troops themselves are too exhausted or demoralized to

---

[1] *Kriegserinnerungen*, p. 351.
[2] This statement was part of a telegram sent from G.H.Q. to the German Foreign Office on October 1.

carry out these orders—then the *army* is no longer a good army; is no longer likely to fight well. In other words we cannot distinguish between the efficiency of an 'army' and the efficiency of the soldiers in it; or rather, if we do make such a distinction, it is not one between two independent things but between two ways of looking at the same thing.

Now one of the main reasons (as we have seen) why in the view of the High Command an armistice became necessary in the autumn of 1918 was that the troops in the German Army were becoming demoralized and could no longer be relied upon. Not indeed all of them. For every hundred soldiers who shouted 'strike breakers' there were at least a hundred, perhaps many more, who were still able and willing to fight bravely. Nevertheless, the proportion of exhausted and demoralized troops was such that the German *Army*, as a whole, was seriously weakened —especially in view of its heavy losses in men and equipment; so seriously weakened that its commanding officers had to admit that there was no longer any hope of achieving victory.

Again that means, if words have any meaning at all, that the German Army was beaten by the autumn of 1918. To revert to the analogy from the boxing ring: if one of the boxer's arms is so weak that he can no longer use it for hitting his opponent; or if his legs are so tired that he is unable to move back in the face of his opponent's attacks; then that may be an explanation of *how* he came to lose the fight—it does not alter the fact that he did lose the fight. We should not take seriously the argument that after all he, the boxer, remained undefeated in the ring, having merely been betrayed by his left arm or his right leg! Yet an exactly similar argument was taken extremely seriously during the twenties and thirties as applied to the German Army in 1918. For this there were two reasons. First the desire of the professional soldiers, from Hindenburg downwards, to dissociate themselves from any share in the blame for Germany's defeat. For them 'the Army' had always meant the officer corps, the hard centre and kernel of the fighting organism, with its traditions and its corps spirit and its code of soldierly honour; and when they set out to defend the Army they were really defending themselves. Put in plain language, their argument ran: 'The German Army's defeat was due to demoralization among the troops, to lack of support from home, to any one of a hundred other factors: it was *not* due to mistakes by the German military leadership.' In other words, the boxer lost because his arms or legs gave in—or because he had inferior gloves or shoes—or because he had not had enough beef-steak during his period of training; but throughout the contest his *brain* continued to work perfectly and would have carried him through for at least another round or two if the other parts of his body had only held out!

And secondly, of course, the concept of an unbeaten army was an invaluable tool in the hands of all who were preparing and working for a Second World War. Tell a boxer that he was not *really* beaten in his last fight and he will be that much more willing to enter the ring a second time; that much less doubtful of victory when the bell sounds for the first round.

The conclusion is inescapable: the German Army *was* beaten in the First World War in the only relevant or significant sense of that word. One can explain and even excuse that fact in many different ways; what one cannot do is to deny it—for it is a straight historical fact.

5.

Granted, then, that the German Army was beaten in the First World War—even if it was saved by the armistice from the impending knock-out blow—what were the reasons for its failure? We come here to the second stage in the stab-in-the-back theory—the contention that the defeat of the German Army was due not to the action of the enemy in the field but to a failure on the part of the homeland.

Not, indeed, that the exponents of the theory claim that this failure was the sole cause of Germany's downfall. They are also ready to adduce other explanations; in particular, the effects of the British blockade and the defection of Germany's allies. But we need not linger over these. Undoubtedly they both played a part in bringing about the final catastrophe: the former by depriving Germany of vital raw materials, by forcing her to adopt all sorts of labour-wasting devices for the production of substitutes, and (not least) by cutting her off from overseas food-supplies; the latter by placing an intolerable strain on the German Army's man-power resources. Many German writers have dilated on the blockade as an unfair form of warfare— though not (so far as I know) in connexion with its use against England in the U-boat war. They have also sought comfort in denouncing Germany's allies for deserting her before the end. Whether there is any justification in these strictures does not concern us here.[1] All that need be noted is, once again, that to explain Germany's defeat by these considerations is not to explain it away. They help to show that the defeat was not discreditable to Germany, and that is admittedly important. But they do not disprove the *fact* of defeat.

The stab-in-the-back explanation of the defeat is of a very different significance. It sets out to save the reputation of the German Army at the expense, not of a foreign nation, whether enemy or ally, but of Germany itself. Two groups of people inside Germany are accused in different versions of the theory of having betrayed the Army. Sometimes it is said that the home *Government* let the *High Command* down; sometimes that the home *Public* let the *Army* down.

The only argument which has ever been put forward (so far as I know) for the first of these two versions of the theory refers to the events of October 1918, described above. Up till then there had been no suggestion of any conflict between the two— on the contrary Germany's military leaders were able to boast that Germany, unlike the western democracies, was a military State, in which the Civilian Government was, in war-time, completely subordinated to the Army. Our examination of what happened in the last six weeks of war shows that then, too, the Civilian Government only applied for an armistice when the High Command asked and indeed insisted that it should do so. There can be no question of a stab-in-the-back here.

Then was it the German people who failed? Certainly, in a sense it did fail, though only to a limited extent. After four years of war, privations, and constantly deferred hopes, it was tired and depressed; longed, above all, for the war to end.[2] This atmosphere in due course spread to the front—carried by letters and by soldiers returning from leave. As we shall see in a moment, however, this factor was certainly not responsible for the poor spirits of the front-line troops, which rested on far

---

[1] We return to the question of the blockade in Chapter II.

[2] See on this Meinecke, 'Die deutsche Novemberrevolution', reprinted in his book *Staat und Persönlichkeit*. The politically conscious, and active, minority on the left had in addition to more general factors been discouraged by the blatant imperialism of the Treaties of Brest-Litovsk and Bucharest (see below, pp. 40–1), as also by the failure of the Kaiser's Government to carry out any of its promised democratic reforms.

firmer foundations than an occasional discouraging letter from
home. And in any case it is a fantastically inadequate ground
for talking of a 'stab-in-the-back'.

The truth of the matter is that by and large the morale of
the home population was higher throughout the closing stages
of the war than was the morale of the troops at the front. True,
there had been occasional strikes in this or that armaments
factory. But there had also been desertions among the troops—
and desertion is a far more serious step for a soldier than is
striking for a factory worker. Moreover, the soldier at the front
had some opportunity of seeing how things were going: he
knew the force of the Allied offensive; he knew something of
the extent of Germany's losses; he knew, too, from the time of
the German spring offensive how much superior the Allies were
to the German Army in food, clothing, equipment, and guns.[1]
All this was largely hidden from the German civilian. He heard
only what he was told by his leaders. And they, up till the end,
spoke only in terms of successes and imminent victory. If he
had any inkling of the real state of affairs, it came from soldiers
on leave from the front: in other words, the Army infected the
home population with depression and defeatism at least as much
as the home population the Army. But in general the German
civilian did *not* know how badly the war was going. Even the
leaders of the political parties in the Reichstag were kept in
ignorance of the true state of affairs. With the result that when
the final blow came, it was all the more terrible for being so
completely unexpected, and the average German could only
echo in bitterness and bewilderment the words of Heydebrand
in the corridors of the Reichstag: 'We have been deceived and
betrayed.'

Then what *did* the German people do which might justify the
accusation of having stabbed the army in the back?

The mutiny at Kiel was an affair of sailors, not civilians, and
in any case came far too late to affect the outcome of the war.
The Revolution only broke out after it had become known

[1] Several Germans who fought on the western front throughout 1918 have
told me that what discouraged them more than anything else was to discover
the kind of things—leather boots, tins of bully beef, and so on—which the
Allied armies left behind them when they retreated in March and April.
These finds brought home to the German soldier the immense material
resources of his enemies and killed at one blow the official German propaganda line that the Allies were at their last gasp.

that an armistice had been urgently applied for. It was in fact not a cause but an expression of defeat.

The infection of the troops with a spirit of Bolshevism? In so far as that played any part at all in the demoralization of the armies on the west, it came there, not from the homeland, but from the eastern front, and was carried by soldiers who had had opportunities of talking with Russian prisoners and absorbing some of their ideas. It is worth while adding, too, that if there were any truth in the picture of bolshevization as the vehicle of the stab in the back, then the responsibility rests with the German military authorities, who deliberately fostered Bolshevism in Russia by sending Lenin and his associates there from Switzerland, and are thus convicted of having played with a weapon whose potency they did not understand.

The poison of English propaganda? Here I must be personal and dogmatic. I have never believed that propaganda was as powerful a weapon as the National Socialists alleged. Its failures have been far more conspicuous than its successes. It will accomplish nothing by itself; at the most it can draw attention to verifiable facts and appeal to already existing hopes and fears. To quote Mr. Churchill: 'If (Allied) propaganda was effective (in the last war), it was because it awoke an echo in German hearts and stirred misgivings which from the beginning had dwelt there.'[1] We must remember, too, that the opportunities for communicating with an enemy audience were infinitely poorer in the First World War than in the Second; and that such propaganda as could be put out at all was as likely to reach the troops as the home population. The only concrete example of supposed enemy propaganda ever cited by exponents of the stab-in-the-back theory in fact reached neither; I refer to the enunciation of Wilson's Fourteen Points. Whether that was the piece of chicanery it was later made out to be I shall discuss in a later chapter. The point here is that it was addressed to the German Government, and the German people knew little or nothing about it—except perhaps in the form of distorted Government versions—till long after. The idea that the German civilian population, having once heard of the Fourteen Points, turned upon the Army and forced it against its will to lay down its arms will certainly not bear investigation, as any German will agree who can remember the last year of the First World War.

[1] Churchill, *The World Crisis*, vol. iv, p. 543.

I conclude that there is no ground whatever for accusing the German civilian population of having betrayed or sabotaged the German Army in the First World War, whether by demoralization or defeatism, by Bolshevism, by listening to enemy propaganda, or in any other way. Germany was not defeated because her people and army were demoralized; the German people and army were demoralized because, and when, they realized that Germany was defeated. The story of a civilian failure was put about to provide an alibi for the 'authorities of the past' (to use Dr. Eugen Fischer's phrase quoted above). That these people should have spread it abroad assiduously is understandable. What is surprising to a non-German is that the German people itself should have meekly accepted, and indeed passionately believed in, so utterly unwarrantable an aspersion on its own behaviour.

6.

Nevertheless, as we know, by the autumn of 1918 the German civilian population, and still more the Army, was discouraged and depressed. And no doubt this general fatigue contributed to a slowing up of war production at home, as it did to a reduction in the efficiency of the troops at the front. Suppose, now, that these manifestations had not displayed themselves; suppose that the German people had somehow remained as fresh and resilient in 1918 as when the war began, what would the effect have been upon its outcome?

This represents the third and final stage in the stab-in-the-back theory. The propagandists have frequently asserted that if Germany had only held on until the spring of 1919, defeat would have been converted into victory. The argument has a bitter taste to-day; its purpose is by now so transparent—to evoke still higher powers of endurance in the German people than it had displayed in the First World War. Nevertheless, it must be briefly examined and disposed of.

First let us note that at the time nobody, not even Ludendorff or Hindenburg, suggested that if the war had lasted into 1919 it could have ended with victory. All they claimed was that it *might* have led to less unfavourable peace terms—and, as we have seen, the High Command's real hope even of that lay not in actually continuing the war but in being in a position to threaten to do so. The suggestion that defeat could have been *averted* by fighting on is patently and indeed grotesquely false.

Secondly, it is more than questionable whether the Allies would have been taken in by any conference-table bluff, had Germany been in a position to carry it out. I have already pointed out that until the last moment they fully expected the war to continue into 1919; had made all arrangements for delivering a final smashing blow as soon as the winter was over. The allegation that England (or America) was on the point of collapse in 1918 is another obvious falsehood.

Thirdly, the prolongation of the war into the fifth spring, while it would have caused the Allies losses, would have been far more costly for Germany—the weaker side, constantly retreating (perhaps across the frontiers of the Reich itself), nearing the end of her last remaining resources.

And fourthly, the danger was imminent that the German Army would not be able to retreat at all; that by the cutting of the vital railway lines it would be faced with complete isolation.[1]

Once more we come back to the vital military fact: *the German Army was already beaten when the armistice was signed.* Prolonging the war would merely have magnified the disaster; it would uselessly have added to the sum total of human suffering on both sides.

And therefore it was not merely common sense on the part of the Government to call a halt; it would have been irresponsible, criminal folly to have done anything else. The German people doubtless could have held out longer, and would have done so if it had been called upon to. But the effect would merely have been to add unnecessarily to its own burden of misery. A conclusion the force of which is tragically apparent to-day.

The upshot of this long discussion is, then: first, the German Army was beaten in the First World War; secondly, the immediate cause of the defeat was the military superiority of its opponents; thirdly, various factors can be adduced to explain the relatively inferior position of the German Army, among them the effects of the blockade and the defection of Germany's allies, but they do not alter it as a fact; fourthly, a failure of

[1] See above, pp. 6, 8.

nerve among the civilian population is *not* included among these factors; and fifthly, a prolongation of the war into its fifth spring would have been useless and criminal.

In short, the stab-in-the-back theory is from first to last a legend and a myth, put forward by evil men for the concealment of their own mistakes and the furtherance of their aggressive and warlike ends.

II

FROM THE ARMISTICE TO THE PEACE

THE armistice terms were such as largely to nullify Ludendorff's hope of renewing the hostilities at a later date, or at
least of using the threat to do so as a bargaining weapon at the
Peace Conference. German troops were on all fronts withdrawn behind the frontiers of the Reich; in the west they were
withdrawn behind the Rhine, Allied troops occupying the whole
of the left bank of the river and establishing one or two bridge-
heads on the right bank. Effectively the whole of the German
Army's equipment of guns, machine-guns, trench mortars, and
aircraft were surrendered to the victors (Art. 4), along with
thousands of locomotives, railway trucks, and lorries (Art. 7).
Allied prisoners in German hands were released and sent home,
but the Allies retained charge of their German prisoners pending
a peace settlement (Art. 18). The German battle fleet steamed
across the North Sea and gave itself up to the Royal Navy
(Art. 23). (The fact that it scuttled itself at Scapa Flow seemed
at the time a mere empty gesture of defiance—a pointless breach
of the armistice agreements; but as we shall see, it was not
without its significance as an indication of the High Command's
attitude to the armistice.)

Beyond all this it was clearly laid down that Germany would
be called upon to make reparation for damage done by the
German Army to civilian property in the occupied territories
(Art. 19); and that the existing British blockade would remain
in force—though the Allies stated that they envisaged supplying
Germany with foodstuffs while the armistice remained in force
(Art. 26).

These were severe terms. The fact that they were accepted
by Germany indicates how desperate was her need for an
immediate cessation of hostilities. They also meant that Germany's power to hit back if the armistice did not end in peace
was cripplingly reduced.

Nevertheless in two respects the armistice was not severe
enough. It did not include arrangements for handing over to
the Allies Germany's merchant shipping, amounting at the
time to about a million tons. And it made no provision for the

control of Germany's supplies of gold and foreign exchange.
These omissions had heavy consequences for the German people
in the ensuing months.

For as the winter wore on and spring approached, it became
clear that there were people in Germany who had still not
abandoned the Ludendorff plan. Insane as the idea seems now,
when we look back, these people seriously envisaged terminating
the armistice, at a time adjudged suitable to themselves, and
challenging the Allies to re-engage in battle. Presumably they
counted on the Allies being unwilling to take up the challenge,
which would have been intended as a means of securing more
advantageous peace terms. Even so, it was an irresponsible and
indeed criminal course to pursue; it meant calling upon Germany
as a whole to follow the example of the German battle fleet and
destroy itself rather than accept the consequences of the lost war.

For this purpose the High Command needed all the resources
it could find. There was still a German army, though neither
a large nor well armed one. For a short time it might have
shouted defiance at the Allies across the waters of the Rhine.
Germany still had a war industry—desperately cramped by
shortage of materials, unable to rely upon the co-operation of
more than a part of its personnel, since for the most part the
German working classes had rallied to the support of the new
Government and were trying to adjust themselves realistically
and sanely to the new post-war conditions; but at least the
factories and machines were still there, untouched by air attack,
and the armistice conditions had included no demand for them
to be dismantled or put out of commission.

And finally, Germany still had her merchant ships and still
had her reserves of gold.[1] The High Command resolved to hold
on to these assets at all costs—even at the cost of misery and
starvation for the German civilian population.

Now when the Allies in the armistice conditions declared
their intention of supplying Germany with foodstuffs, they
were acknowledging a moral obligation to do all they reasonably
could to prevent unnecessary suffering among enemy peoples.
But there were four obvious limitations to the extent of this
obligation. First, shipping was very scarce—less so, indeed,
than a year previously, since during 1918 the volume of new-

---

[1] These amounted to £120,000,000, i.e. about 2½ milliard gold marks at
the end of the war—more than twice as much as in 1914.

built tonnage had substantially exceeded U-boat sinkings, but still wholly inadequate to meet the exceptional demands upon it. Secondly, so far as food supplies to Europe were concerned, the first duty was obviously to supply the populations of Allied territories, in some of which—particularly where German troops had been in occupation—food conditions were far worse than inside Germany itself. Thirdly, the problem of finance had to be solved. Free distribution of food could be, and was, undertaken in many cases as a last resort,[1] but the funds at the disposal of the Allied Governments were not unlimited, and here again the needs of Allied and liberated territories had an obvious right to priority of treatment. And finally, Germany was still an enemy country, with which the Allies were at war, and the Allied Governments were not unaware that there were those in high places in Germany for whom the war was not yet over and who would give trouble as soon as they saw an opportunity of doing so.

Under these circumstances it could plausibly have been argued—and was indeed argued to some extent—that shipments of food to Germany must wait till they could be carried through on a normal commercial basis after the conclusion of peace. Some French authorities, in particular, asked themselves whether the German Government's monetary resources should not be devoted to restoring the devastated areas of northern France and Belgium rather than for providing relief inside Germany itself. This matter was discussed at length by the Allies after the Armistice. After full consideration the French representatives gave way to British and American pressure and the Allies agreed to supply Germany with food and other necessities, provided that German ships were used for carrying them and German gold for financing them.

On January 15 representatives of the two sides met at Trier to negotiate a renewal of the armistice. The first question to come up was that of payment. The German representatives attempted to persuade the Allies to accept payment in paper marks—a proposal at once rejected by the Allies on the entirely reasonable ground that the mark was already depreciated and might easily depreciate further if the German financial authori-

---

[1] Of the foodstuffs and other necessaries which went to Germany during the spring and summer of 1919, £5,000,000 (100,000,000 gold marks) worth was delivered free of charge.

ties chose to pursue an inflationary policy.[1] It can hardly be supposed that the German representatives expected any other answer. But they showed indignation at the demand for payment in acceptable form, and only on the second day of the conference, January 16, did they come forward with the statement that Germany was prepared to allocate 125 million gold marks in gold and foreign currencies—about a twentieth of the German reserves—for this vital work. This was, of course, not nearly a large enough sum to cover Germany's needs—but the German representatives flatly refused to offer more, nor were they prepared to consent to make available for the purpose German private property in the United States sequestrated for the duration of the war. The German proposal was—quite simply—that the Allies should supply Germany with food free of charge (under the guise of payment by means of credits which could be repudiated or of marks which could be rendered worthless by inflation) while she retained her gold and foreign exchange 'for the reconstruction of Germany's economic life'— i.e. for the rebuilding of the war machine.

Still more striking was the German attitude to the transport question. When the Allied demand that Germany should release her ships for the purpose of European relief was presented to the German representatives they received assurances that the ships would remain German property and that the freight rates paid would not be lower than the rates paid to other nations. Nevertheless the big German shipowners were opposed to the scheme because they hoped to gain greater profits by engaging in ordinary commerce, and the nationalist elements in the Government would not bring pressure on them because they wanted the ships to remain under German control as a potential weapon of war. And though in the end an agreement was reached on the main principles, Germany agreeing to release her ships and gold, yet so many points of detail were left over 'for settlement at a future date' that if either side wished to postpone taking action it had every excuse for doing so.

Now let us note what happened during the following weeks. The agreement at Trier had provided for supplying Germany with up to 270,000 tons of cereals and fats. On the assumption that once the agreement was reached Germany would act promptly the Allies began shipping foodstuffs in non-German

[1] See on the question of inflation below, pp. 86 ff.

vessels to the Netherlands, ready to be sent across the German frontier as soon as Germany fulfilled her side of the Trier agreement. But the German authorities failed to release their ships or to transfer their gold—so the food remained in Rotterdam.

In the middle of February the armistice came up for a further renewal. The question of food supplies once again figured prominently on the agenda. This time the German representatives were even more truculent. They announced in so many words that they considered the supply of foodstuffs to Germany to be their right, whether or not they chose to allow German ships to be used for the purpose of European relief; in other words, they repudiated their own signature to the Trier agreement. The ships went on rotting in German ports, the gold went on collecting dust in the vaults of the Reichsbank, and the German people remained hungry. In Cologne the sight of starving children was too much for the British soldiers, who shared their rations with these victims of the German war lords' fanaticism and the German shipowners' greed.[1]

At last the realists in the German Government asserted themselves against their own internal enemies. On March 14, more than four months after the armistice, a new and final agreement was made in Brussels between Germany and the Allies. A week later the first ship left Germany on its errand of mercy and before the end of the month foodstuffs were flowing in through German ports in a steady and growing stream. From then on imports of food were limited only by the available shipping and finance.[2]

[1] The full story of the negotiations is to be found in Volume I of the official German Report, *Der Waffenstillstand 1918–1919*, published in Berlin in 1928. See also Bernhard Menne, *Armistice and Germany's Food Supply, 1918–19*. It is obvious that Erzberger, the chief German delegate, was in an extremely difficult position throughout these tortuous negotiations. He had agreed in principle to the idea that giving up German gold and putting German ships into the international shipping pool were a small price to pay for preventing starvation in Germany—and had been called a traitor for his pains. He was apparently not strong enough to stand up to his nationalist and big business critics—so in the March conference he fell into line with the irreconcilables. That did not save him from assassination by his implacable nationalist enemies.

[2] Even in March the French delegates to the Peace Conference endeavoured to oppose the use of Germany's gold reserves for the purchase of food for the civilian population. But once again they were overborne. See on this Lloyd George, *Truth about the Peace Treaties*, pp. 293 ff. We are entitled to blame the French for their intransigence in this whole issue—not merely on humanitarian grounds, but also because (as was pointed out to them by Lloyd George

The distribution of the imported food was left exclusively to the German authorities, the Allies concerning themselves only with seeing that the distribution as between occupied and unoccupied portions of the Reich was in accordance with the needs of the populations concerned. How did the German authorities carry out their task? So far as breadstuffs were concerned they did their work promptly and efficiently. There was no reason why they should not. Germany's shortage of grain was essentially a short-run difficulty; by the summer and the lifting of Germany's own grain harvests the crisis would in any case be past, and she could hope to be once again reasonably self-supporting. But with fats it was otherwise. If Germany was to resume hostilities she must have a stock of fats. And therefore when bacon and edible oils were imported into Germany as a result of the Brussels agreement, a substantial proportion of it was held back. It was not until June, when the authorities finally decided to accept the fact of defeat, that their interest in accumulating fats reserves evaporated.[1] And by June their stocks were so large that they were able at once to double the fats ration for the German people. Thus for nearly three months German adults and children were kept short of a vital foodstuff, which was already available for distribution in German warehouses, because the military leaders who still had effective control over their destinies were still, even then, looking for ways of breaking the armistice and resuming the struggle.

The threat of immediate starvation was not, however, the only problem. If Germany was not merely to obtain imports at once, but to maintain a flow of imports on a long-run basis, she had to find means for the continuous replenishment of her foreign assets. In other words, she had to rebuild her export trade. But this depended on the importation of raw materials. How was this to be done? In April the Allies agreed (though the war was not yet over) that she should be authorized to import all needed types of raw materials up to 50 per cent. of her imports before the war. Instead of accepting this and making arrangements with the suppliers for financing this on a

and President Wilson at the time), if they wanted to obtain reparation from Germany, it was in their own interest to see that Germany did not starve. The vital thing, however, is that the French point of view was never accepted by the Allies as a whole: the delays in the arrival of the food were the responsibility not of Frenchmen but of Germans.

[1] Temperley, *History of the Peace Conference of Paris*, vol. i, p. 319.

commercial basis (which would certainly have been possible, though difficult), the German authorities demanded a loan from the Allied Governments of £200 millions (4 milliard gold marks) to cover the cost of these imports. The Allies had other things to do with their money than lend it to an enemy country, and the whole scheme fell to the ground. Next the Allies, as a purely business proposition, offered a million pounds' worth of raw materials for setting the Ruhr coalfield in working order. This was in the Allied interest since a substantial part of the coal produced could be transferred to the Allies for use in northern France and Lorraine. But it was also in the interests of the Ruhr workers, to whom it would have given secure employment and a speedier return to peace-time industrial conditions. The German authorities, however, rejected this plan on financial grounds and it too was dropped. Finally the Allies offered to authorize Germany to import from neutral countries raw materials for which she had already paid. The German authorities killed this plan too by demanding a guarantee that these raw materials would be allowed through the blockade even if the Peace Treaty were rejected and hostilities renewed. Again German policy was dominated by the Ludendorff principle: whatever the cost to German industry and the civilian population, do not sacrifice any assets which might be useful for the purpose of continuing—or threatening to continue—the war! But the result was in this case merely to postpone any importations from overseas of industrial raw materials until after the peace had been signed. By their fanatical refusal to face the fact of defeat, by their determination to keep open the possibility of renewing hostilities, the nationalist elements who were still in effective control of Germany's relations with the outside world obstructed the process of recovery and restoration inside Germany, without in any way benefiting even their own longer-run plans.

But so far as foodstuffs and other immediate necessaries of civilian life were concerned, as we have seen, these elements were at last overborne. With the result that by the end of August, Germany had received, under Allied auspices alone, more than a million tons of foodstuffs and more than a hundred thousand tons of clothing, soap, and medical supplies. This was a larger total than went to any other country in the whole of Europe. In addition Austria received more than half a million tons of supplies. Of the total supplies sent by the Allies to their friends and enemies in Europe during the ten months following the armistice, over one-third found their way to Germany and Austria.[1] To which must be added food imports from neutral countries. These were authorized by the Allies to an unlimited extent, in spite of the blockade, as soon as the German authorities had withdrawn their opposition to the use of their ships and their gold for relief purposes.

In the light of all this, what are we to say of the story, so widely circulated by the friends of war in Germany, that the Allies sadistically maintained the 'hunger blockade' long after the war was over? The answer is clear and crushing. First, the war was not over for these people—they were later to proclaim arrogantly that for them it had never stopped and that the whole period from 1918 till 1939 was just a long pause for breath.[2] Secondly, even though it was not over, the Allies accepted the principle of supplying foodstuffs and other necessaries to the German people. Thirdly, they carried that principle into effect as soon as the German authorities, after four weary months, released their gold and their shipping for buying and transporting it. And fourthly, the reason why the German authorities held their gold and their shipping back was because they were thinking in terms of continuing, at whatever cost to the German civilian population, the already lost war.

[1] For the purpose of making this comparison I have of course not included the foodstuffs sold by the United States on a purely commercial basis to Britain, France, and Italy.
[2] See on this below, Chapter V.

III

THE PEACE TREATY

1.

AT last, on June 28, the peace was signed, the blockade machinery was formally scrapped two weeks later (for months it had had no operative significance), and though relief work and governmental shipments of food to various European countries, including Germany and Austria, were to continue for a further four years, yet the world tried to settle down to peace-time conditions and normal economic relationships. Germany was now no longer an enemy nation. But she was, of course, not recognized as an equal partner with the Allies in the organization of the post-war world. She had obligations to fulfil under the terms of the armistice and the peace; she had to live down the bitterness which had been aroused against her in her former enemies by over four years of war; above all she had to convince the Allies that she cherished no further aggressive or warlike plans, and they for their part had to ensure that she should not be in a position to put any such plans into effect.

Many Germans, even at the time, regarded the attitude of the Allies towards Germany as unfair and humiliating. Their standpoint seems to have been that, once the peace had been signed, Germany should at once have been admitted into the circle of Great Powers on a basis of complete equality of rights. This was a wholly unrealistic attitude—as any German can see for himself if he puts the proposition round the other way and considers what his attitude would have been towards France at the present moment if the Second World War had ended with a German victory in the summer of 1940. Even if his rulers had been working towards a new world order based on international co-operation (and they would not have been) he, and they, would have regarded it as laughable to suppose that a defeated ex-enemy should at once be recognized as having an equal say with a victorious Germany in the day-to-day conduct of world affairs. What is astonishing in the history of the post-war years was the speed with which public opinion and even governmental policy among the Allies, as a whole, veered round in favour of Germany—a fact which, indeed, had disastrous consequences for the prospects of an enduring peace.

But that is a subject for future chapters. At the moment what concerns us is the fact that Germany came to the peace negotiations at Versailles as a defeated Power, in no position to bargain with her enemies and with no claim, either then or for years to come, to be treated as an equal partner in working out the settlement.

In this sense—and in this sense only—the Treaty of Versailles was a 'dictated' peace. It was imposed on Germany in so far as she had in practice no option but to accept its terms. Legally and formally her representatives could have refused to agree; and indeed, as we know, there were elements with great influence inside Germany who were in favour of taking this course. But the consequences of carrying out any such policy would have been completely disastrous for Germany, and in the end she swallowed her pride and agreed—not, admittedly, of her own free will, but from hard necessity.

To say, however, that the Treaty of Versailles was a 'dictated' peace is not at all the same thing as saying that it was an *unjust* peace. In subsequent years propagandists inside Germany—and in the outside world too, for that matter—made effective use of this confusion; so much so that to the ordinary German the phrase 'dictated peace' came to be a catchword synonym of supposed injustices and oppressions arbitrarily imposed upon a helpless Germany by ruthless and implacable enemies. It is sufficient answer to this to point out that even absolute dictators *can* behave justly towards their subjects; and so too victors *can* behave justly towards their defeated enemies even in an 'imposed' peace settlement. The question whether the Treaty of Versailles was or was not a just peace can only be settled by examining its provisions and finding out whether they were harsher than Germany was entitled to expect.

Now there are two ways in which the Treaty of Versailles might, in principle, be proved unjust. One is if it can be shown to have contravened pledges earlier given by the Allies to Germany—particularly if those pledges played any part in deciding Germany to lay down her arms. The other is if it can be shown that its provisions were in themselves unduly severe and onesided. The propagandists have made great play with both these lines of argument. They have said, first, that Ger-

many consented to an armistice on the basis of President Wilson's
Fourteen Points, which were then cynically thrown over and
forgotten once she was helpless; and secondly, that the Treaty
was intolerably harsh towards Germany in that it (1) saddled
Germany with the sole responsibility for having caused the war;
(2) imposed unilateral disarmament; (3) lopped off vital German
territories from the body of the Reich; (4) deprived Germany of
her colonies; and (5) imposed a crushing burden of reparations
payments. Let us examine these two sets of assertions in turn.

2.

The Fourteen Points were enunciated by President Wilson
in a speech on January 8, 1918. They represented his picture
of how the world should be reshaped after the war was over.
In that sense they were a declaration of American policy. We
shall come to an analysis of their contents a little later; for the
moment it is sufficient to mention the fundamental principle on
which they were based—the principle of national self-determination. It was American policy, said President Wilson, that no
European State should control territories inhabited by peoples
of foreign race or nationality; only if each European people
were left free to govern itself could there be any hope of an
enduring peace.[1]

As such the Fourteen Points expressed only the American
standpoint, and it has sometimes been said that they were
never accepted by the other Allies. In fact they were doubtless
not accepted by Italy, which had entered the war in 1915 with
certain specific objectives in view—namely the acquisition of
the South Tyrol and Italia Irredenta from the Austro-Hungarian
Empire (and world recognition of her sovereignty over the
Dodecanese Islands, which she had captured from Turkey in
1912)—and Italy had been promised these by the Allies as a
condition of her entering the war. But France and Britain,
though not formally aligning themselves with America in this
issue till much later, were undoubtedly in sympathy with the
spirit and approach to the problem offered by the Fourteen
Points; indeed in many questions the Fourteen Points simply

[1] The Fourteen Points contain a number of important exceptions to this
principle, as we shall see. But in general they adhere closely to its spirit—too
closely, in fact; for Wilson was unquestionably oversimplifying when he
supposed that Europe's problems could be solved merely by the universal
application of his 'right to national self-determination'.

echoed an authoritative declaration of Allied war aims which had been issued in January 1917 shortly before America came into the war.

Thus the Fourteen Points were rightly taken at the time to be a declaration, in general terms, of Allied intentions for the post-war world—intentions which might be and were modified in detail later on but which constituted, so to speak, a directive for the Allied Powers when they came to plan the peace.

On the other hand, they were certainly not a formal 'peace offer' to the Central Powers. In the first place they were not addressed to Germany and her allies nor formally communicated to them. Secondly, though they contained (as we shall see) certain concrete proposals for post-war Europe, they were to a large extent vague and theoretical and they were certainly not exhaustive. There was thus no question of the American President's saying to the German Government 'if Germany will agree to this, that, and the other specific proposal, then America will be ready to make peace and in all other respects Germany will be left free to act as she pleases'.

Nevertheless, Germany was entitled to assume that if she were to express her acceptance of the Fourteen Points there would be a prima facie case for opening peace discussions. In that sense the Fourteen Points constituted, at the time at least, a potential peace offer.

The German Government did not, however, declare its acceptance of the Fourteen Points. On the contrary, it treated them with ridicule. Germany was at the time doing well in the war. The campaign in the east was practically over, the spring offensive in the west was being planned, the High Command believed it could force the way through to final victory by the summer. And the German rulers were not interested in a peace by negotiation—still less in a peace based on the principle of self-determination. This they displayed clearly in the treaties they imposed on Russia and Rumania that spring. By the Treaty of Brest-Litovsk Russia, in addition to a huge reparations payment, was forced to give up 34 per cent. of her population, 32 per cent. of her agricultural land, 54 per cent. of her industrial undertakings, and 89 per cent. of her coal-mines. Germany took control of the whole of Poland, Lithuania, Latvia, and Estonia, and set up puppet governments in Finland, the Ukraine, and Georgia under direct and open

German control, thereby cutting Russia off from the Black Sea and almost from the Baltic Sea as well. The Treaty was in fact one of naked imperialism; it represented the apotheosis of the 'push to the east' which had for so long been the dream of one school of German expansionists.

The peace imposed on Rumania two months later followed the same general pattern. To Austria-Hungary she lost the Carpathian range; the southern Dobrudja went to Bulgaria; the northern Dobrudja right up to the northernmost mouth of the Danube was put under a German-Austrian condominium, so that Rumania was cut off from the sea; and the vital Rumanian oilwells were handed over to Germany for exclusive exploitation for ninety-nine years.

One point is worth recording in this connexion. When the negotiations for peace with Russia were first contemplated, the Central Powers accepted and announced the formula of 'no annexations, no indemnities, and the principle of self-determination' as the basis on which they would conclude peace. This was announced before the end of 1917—that is to say, before the publication of the Fourteen Points. It was intended partly to impress the Western Powers with Germany's moderation and partly to put an end to further Russian resistance. Whether it was taken seriously by the German Chancellor Hertling is not clear. It certainly was not taken seriously by Hindenburg and Ludendorff. Nor did the fact that Germany had committed herself to it prevent them from insisting that when the time came 'a victor's peace should crown a victor's war'. Not merely that, but the Germans stiffened their terms during the actual course of negotiations. In the first draft of the Treaty the Russian-German frontier was fixed to reach the Baltic Sea just east of Riga. But as the discussions proceeded, the greed of the German imperialists increased as they realized the complete helplessness of their enemies, and it was then that they added northern Latvia and Estonia to their spoils; it was then, too, that they forced Russia to renounce sovereignty over Finland, the Ukraine, and Georgia.

Clearly the makers of the Treaties of Brest-Litovsk and Bucharest were not inspired by considerations of justice or fair dealing or by respect for their own earlier undertakings. Yet one German paper acclaimed the Treaty with Russia as evidence that 'the German Government has worked only for a peace of understanding and consideration'. The Austrian Chancellor Baron Burian described the Treaty of Bucharest as 'moderate and just'. The *Münchener Post* declared, in the first flush of triumph, that it was 'a model of the peace to be imposed on all our enemies'. And it is related that a German staff officer, in reply to the protests of a Rumanian diplomat at its terms, said: 'You call this a *harsh* peace? Just wait till you see what we are preparing for France and England!'[1]

To many people in Germany, however, the treaties came as a great shock. Workers came out on strike against the settlement with Russia, members of the Reichstag denounced its brutality and stupidity; and Hitler, at a much later date, had to record how his attempts to stir up popular resentment against the Versailles Treaty were in the immediate post-war years met by the cry: 'And Brest-Litovsk?'[2] But their protests went unheeded. How far they expressed the view of the majority in Germany it is impossible, after this lapse of time, to ascertain. If, as I believe, the number of Germans was very large who were either explicitly opposed to Germany's policy in the east or while acquiescing were deeply uneasy about its consequences, then we can legitimately say that the Treaties of Brest-Litovsk and Bucharest were a triumph for the German ruling class, not merely over Germany's external enemies, but also over the German people.

And if many in Germany were shocked, still more was the world outside. The effect on neutral countries was enormous and may well have contributed to the decision of many of them to join the war on the side of the Allies. To the peoples of the Allied countries, and particularly to the Americans, the treaties came as a blinding ray of light. They for the first time really understood what they were fighting against and put aside once and for all any thought of a compromise peace. Until then the United States had not been whole-hearted in her prosecution of the war. Many Americans were inclined to wonder whether they were not perhaps being used to further a cause which was not theirs. From now on there was no doubt. Nor was there any doubt of the significance of Brest-Litovsk in the mind of

---

[1] I have been unable to find the original source of this story, which may therefore be apocryphal. But it unquestionably reflects the attitude of the German ruling caste at the time, when the offensive in the west was still going well.   [2] *Mein Kampf*, p. 519.

President Wilson. In a speech at Baltimore on April 16 he said:

'I am ready to discuss a fair and just and honest peace at any time that it is sincerely proposed. But the answer, when I proposed such a peace, came from the German commanders in Russia, and I cannot mistake the meaning of the answer. I accept the challenge. Germany has once more said that force, and force alone, shall decide. . . . There is therefore but one response possible from us: force, force to the utmost, force without stint or limit, the righteous and triumphant force which shall make Right the law of the world.'

Thus the policy of the High Command in the east finally united the world against Germany and made it certain that the war would continue until she was defeated. Those Germans were entirely right who felt that it was stupid as well as brutal.

Note, however, that President Wilson did not, even then, renounce the principles he had laid down in the Fourteen Points. Had these constituted a 'peace offer' he would have had every right to do so—for the Treaties of Brest-Litovsk and Bucharest were as flat and contemptuous a rejection of their principles as could well be imagined.[1] But as they were not a peace offer but a statement of American—and more generally, of Allied— intentions, they still stood. With one important qualification. From then on it was clear to the President—and was constantly reiterated by him in his speeches—that no peace with Germany would be possible, whether on the basis of the Fourteen Points or on any other basis, until the existing rulers of Germany had been once and for all eliminated; and that meant, as he now realized, until Germany had been decisively beaten in the field of battle.

At the time the High Command remained blandly and blindly indifferent to the effects of their eastern policy on the outside world. But six months later came the day of reckoning. When, on October 12, the German Government in its dire need for an armistice communicated to the American President that Germany was now at last ready to accept the principles of the

[1] The propagandists in Germany regularly overlooked this point. The more they insisted the Fourteen Points were a 'peace offer' the less plausible became their own assertion that Germany, ten months later, was 'tricked' into accepting it. The dilemma is in fact inescapable: either the Fourteen Points were a peace offer—in which case Germany rejected it and it was not renewed; or else they were *not* a peace offer—in which case there could be no question of a 'breach of faith' even if the Allies subsequently abandoned them.

Fourteen Points, Wilson answered in so many words that the conditions for granting an armistice would be left to the Allied military authorities and that it was no use appealing to him— or to the Fourteen Points—over their heads. Three and a half weeks later, when the German armistice plenipotentiaries were received by Marshal Foch and tried to raise questions concerning more long-run issues, they were informed at once that the Allied Commander-in-Chief was not empowered to discuss any such matters. He read out to them a statement of the terms on which the Allies were prepared to grant an armistice—a statement in which no reference of any kind to the Fourteen Points occurred—and the German plenipotentiaries accepted those terms.

This point deserves careful notice. It is possible—I do not say likely—that if Germany's policy towards her beaten enemies in March and May had not openly flaunted the principles which the Fourteen Points set out to embody, the Allies might have agreed to introduce a reference to the Fourteen Points in the armistice terms. But by October they were perfectly well aware of the sort of people with whom they had to deal. It was not that the Allies doubted the sincerity of the German official conversion to the Fourteen Points; they *knew*, for certain, that there had been no such conversion. These were the sort of men who flouted principles when in prosperity to which they eagerly appealed with a great show of earnestness on the day of adversity; men who had shown in their dealings with Russia and Rumania that their professions of belief in fair dealing and 'conciliation' were nothing but an empty sham—or rather were a deliberate device for confusing and hoodwinking their opponents; men who in their hearts believed in force and force only. Those men had to be eliminated by force—only then could Europe settle down to rebuilding itself on a basis of justice and national self-determination. On this issue the attitude of the Allies was made perfectly clear. The suggestion, therefore, that Germany laid down her arms in November 1918 on the basis of the Fourteen Points is in direct contradiction to the facts. Germany laid down her arms because her military situation was hopeless and was rapidly becoming catastrophic, and because, as Hindenburg had told Erzberger before he left for Compiègne, any terms must be accepted that the Allies chose to demand.

But that did *not* mean that the Allies had changed their mind as to the nature of the final peace settlement. The distinction here between armistice terms and peace terms is of vital importance. The former determined the actual cessation of hostilities. From the Allied point of view the paramount consideration there was the need to see to it that Germany was rendered militarily impotent, and the fact that Germany was ready to accept those terms was thus the expression of the completeness of her defeat. But the peace terms were concerned with the rebuilding of Europe—if possible of a better and more stable Europe than had bred the war four years earlier. And on *that* issue President Wilson retained his faith in the Fourteen Points. Moreover, early in October he received a communication from Britain and the other Allies informing him that they too accepted the Fourteen Points as providing the groundwork on which a just and lasting peace might be built, though they made three reservations which the American President willingly or unwillingly accepted.[1]

So in spite of all that happened in the meantime the Allies met Germany at the Versailles Conference Table pledged in their own minds to make a settlement in conformity with the general spirit of the Fourteen Points. Once again let it be stressed that no promise had been made to *Germany* to this effect, nor had the possibility of any such promise been offered to Germany as an inducement to her to lay down her arms. But in their own minds the Allies were clear as to the kind of peace they wished and hoped to achieve—and it was the kind of peace which Wilson had sketched out on January 8, 1918. Our next question is, therefore, how far did the Treaty of Versailles embody those hopes—how far was it a fair and genuine expression of the spirit of the Fourteen Points?

3.

Of all the hundreds of thousands of people who have at one time or another denounced the Treaty of Versailles as a monstrous betrayal of President Wilson's principles, I suppose only a small percentage have had any clear idea of what the

---

[1] For details of the reservations see the Appendix, where the text of the Fourteen Points is reprinted in full. Only one of the three concerned Germany, namely that dealing with reparations. On this see below, pp. 60 ff., and next chapter.

Fourteen Points contained, and an even minuter percentage have ever read the actual words in which they were expressed.[1] I have, therefore, thought it worth while to append to this book the full text of the Fourteen Points as originally enunciated by the American President, along with the modifications introduced by the other Allies in October 1918. I hope that my readers will study this Appendix. What they find there will surprise them.

Of the Fourteen Points only three directly concern Germany and German territory at all; namely, Point 5, dealing with colonies; Point 8, dealing with the restoration of France; and Point 13, dealing with the question of Poland.

Of the other eleven, five are of a purely general nature and are designed to indicate a framework for the new world order as a whole (Nos. 1, 2, 3, 4, and 14). The remaining six are concerned with different parts of Europe and the Near East and only involve Germany in so far as they provide for the 'evacuation' and the 'restoration' of the areas concerned.

Germans might, however, in addition claim a contingent and sentimental interest in Points 8 and 9, which deal with the future of the Austro-Hungarian Empire.

The three points directly bearing on Germany are not at all 'favourable' to her in the sense in which that word came to be understood by the propagandists. Germany is *not* promised the return of her colonies; she is called upon to return Alsace-Lorraine and so to right 'the wrong done to France by Prussia in 1871'; and she is to acquiesce in the setting up of 'an independent Polish State' enjoying 'a free and secure access to the sea'.

The question of the 'evacuation' of non-German territories by German troops was academic by the time the Peace Conference assembled, since it had already been carried into effect under the terms of the armistice. Wilson's demand for their 'restoration', on the other hand, was as it stood so vague as to be almost meaningless. But the other Allies made it clear in their rider on this subject that they envisaged 'compensation by Germany for all damage done to the civilian population of

---

[1] According to Prince Max of Baden (*Memoirs*, vol, ii, p. 24), even the German Supreme Command 'had probably no clear idea at first as to the fateful conditions to which the Fourteen Points must in any case commit Germany'.

the Allies and their property'. Whether this represented the American President's original meaning is doubtful but irrelevant. The point is that this rider was accepted by America before hostilities ceased and was incorporated verbatim both in a note sent by Wilson to the German Government on November 5 and in Article 19 of the armistice terms. Thus the principle of reparations was not merely embodied in the modified version of the Fourteen Points which formed the basis of Allied intentions for the peace settlement, but was also accepted by Germany as one of the conditions for the armistice.

Finally a word on the two points concerning Austria-Hungary, though these are not relevant to the Treaty of Versailles, which was concerned only with Germany. Point 9 provided for a readjustment of the frontier between Italy and Austria-Hungary 'along clearly recognizable lines of nationality'; Point 10 for according to the various peoples of Austria-Hungary 'the freest opportunity of autonomous development'. This latter provision clearly implied, though it did not specifically say so, that Austria too should be free and autonomous. On the subject of a possible future union of Austria with Germany it expressed no clear view either way. Point 9, if it had been allowed to stand, would certainly not have permitted the incorporation in Italy of the Austrians of South Tyrol and of the Slav populations in the districts east and south of Trieste. But the Italian Government had made a specific and clear reservation on these matters before the conclusion of the armistice, basing its case on the Treaty with Britain and France which had brought her into the war in 1915. And this reservation was accepted and recognized by Italy's Allies before they came to negotiate the Treaty of St. Germain.[1]

[1] See the *Intimate Papers of Colonel House*, vol. iv, p. 178. It should be noted that in the case of Austria, as of Germany, there was no question of a change of policy after Austria had been 'tricked' into surrender. Austria surrendered unconditionally on November 3 without waiting for the other Allies to declare their adherence to the Fourteen Points, and knowing perfectly well—for the Italians had never tried to conceal it—that one of Italy's main war aims was to push her northern frontier up to the Brenner Pass.

I may add that a month earlier, when the Austro-Hungarian Government first asked the American President for peace on the basis of the Fourteen Points, they were specifically warned (in Wilson's note of October 8) that the former subject peoples of the Empire, viz. the Czechoslovaks and the Jugoslavs, were to be 'the judges of what action on the part of the Austro-Hungarian Government will satisfy their aspirations and their conception of their rights and destiny as members of the family of nations'. The relevance

Thus a study of the terms—as opposed to the myth—of the Fourteen Points shows that they offered Germany no easy prospects, no high-flown promises, no undertaking to forget the past and let bygones be bygones. Germany might reasonably hope in due course to be accepted into the comity of nations and enjoy the benefits of the proposed new world order. But there was no suggestion that that could be accorded to her at once, and for the rest she was faced with at least a possibility of losing her colonies and with the certainty of having to make territorial concessions on her eastern and western frontiers and of paying reparations. The Fourteen Points were certainly not calculated to provide an unwary Germany with a bait whereby she might be trapped into laying down her arms before she needed to.

How far, then, were the principles of the Fourteen Points, as modified by agreement with the other Allies before the armistice, carried over into the Treaty? We need not spend long on this matter, because once it is realized what the pre-armistice proposals of the Allies really were, the propagandists' contention that the Treaty of Versailles constituted a betrayal of *these proposals*, loses its sting; interest shifts rather to the justice, or injustice, of the Treaty on its own merits. Let us rapidly survey the main points at issue.

The territorial adjustments effected by the Treaty were almost without exception precisely what the Fourteen Points had envisaged.

Germany lost Alsace-Lorraine to France. But when the French authorities proposed the detachment of the whole area west of the Rhine, on grounds of strategical security, their demand was flatly refused by the other Allies—because it conflicted with the principles underlying the Fourteen Points.

On the east Germany gave up extensive territories to the newly formed Poland. The demarcation of the actual frontier between Germany and Poland raised many difficulties. Some of these were settled—I do not say solved—by plebiscites of the population concerned. The result was that considerable areas were included in the Reich which had been provisionally assigned to Poland by the Expert Commission charged with making proposals for the new frontier on the basis of the

of this pronouncement for the Sudetenland problem is obvious. Cf. below, pp. 146 f.

principles of self-determination and strategic security. The most striking case was that of Upper Silesia. There a substantial majority of the population was undoubtedly Polish—and Point 13 demanded that the new Polish State should include all areas inhabited by 'indisputably Polish populations'. But on Germany's request a plebiscite was held there to find out the wishes of the population; and when the population of Upper Silesia voted in favour of Germany their decision was accepted. Here, therefore, was an instance in which one of the Fourteen Points was overruled *in favour of Germany*—as a result of applying the principle of local self-determination.

The other main problem, so far as Poland was concerned, was also solved in a way which was more generous to Germany than the Fourteen Points called for. Point 13 specifically promised Poland a free and secure access to the sea. The obvious point of access was at the mouth of the Vistula, since the territory immediately south thereof—what the Germans called Eastern Pomerania and/or West Prussia—was inhabited predominantly by Poles and was due to be incorporated in Poland anyway. But Danzig was an indisputably German city. Here was a second case of a straight conflict between the terms of the Fourteen Points and the underlying principle of self-determination. No charge of betraying *the Fourteen Points* could have been brought against the Allies if they had assigned Danzig to Poland. As it was they tried to make the best of both worlds by setting up Danzig as a Free City. Alas, they merely succeeded in falling between two stools! Neither the application of the Fourteen Points nor—still less—the worship of the principle of self-determination provided them with the panacea for Europe's ills which they were seeking. But that the Versailles settlement of the Polish question was an honest attempt to carry out the Allies' pre-armistice intentions is beyond doubt. It failed because neither President Wilson nor his colleagues among the other Allies fully grasped the complexity of the problem to be solved.

In three cases Germany had, by the Treaty, to consent to cessions of territory not specifically provided for by the Fourteen Points. Two of these—Danish Schleswig and the Eupen-Malmedy area on the frontier of Belgium—were settled on the basis of the principle of self-determination. The third, that of the Saar territory, came under a different head. France required the use of the Saar coal for supplying the blast furnaces of Lorraine and as a temporary replacement for the coal-mines of northern France which had been put out of action by the German Army before it left French soil. Her claim therefore rested on the right to reparation for damage done. But the population of the area was unquestionably German and to have incorporated it in Metropolitan France would have been a clear breach of the self-determination principle. So the Saar territory was put temporarily under the control of an International Commission on the understanding that it would revert to Germany sixteen years later if the inhabitants showed by plebiscite that they so desired. Again a compromise between two conflicting elements in President Wilson's vision of the post-war world—but this time a compromise which worked tolerably well, though it can of course be argued that other and better solutions of the Saar problem might have been found.

Germany was by the Treaty of Versailles deprived of her colonies. This decision was taken in entire conformity with the Fourteen Points. Point 5 laid down merely that in considering colonial claims due weight should be attached to the 'interests of the populations concerned' as well as to the 'equitable claims of the Government whose title is to be determined'. The case was argued at length before the signing of the Treaty, the claims of the Allied Governments for security being weighed against those of Germany for 'a place in the sun', and in the end Germany's case was rejected. Whether this was a just decision *on its merits* is a matter to which we shall return. But it was a decision which was at the least foreshadowed as a possibility in the Fourteen Points, and it provides no case whatever for a charge of breach of faith or betrayal on the part of the makers of the Treaty.

Germany was called upon to pay a high bill in reparations. The question of the *merits* of the reparations clauses in the Treaty is again one which must be postponed. But in attempting to assess the amount of reparations to be exacted, the Allies were guided strictly by the principle of ascertaining 'the damage done to the civilian population of the Allies and their property'. On only one point were they guilty of a certain degree of sharp practice—namely when the British representatives persuaded their colleagues to include in the bill a charge for pensions and reparation allowances for the dependants of fighting soldiers, and thereby enabled Great Britain and the British Dominions to claim a share in the reparations proceeds. This was clearly *not* envisaged in the reparations clause of the modified Fourteen Points and represents therefore a case in which the Treaty departed from the Allies' previously announced policy. As it turned out, however, the matter was one of little practical importance since even without this item the Reparations Bill would have been more than Germany could have paid—and of course very much more than in the event she did pay.[1]

With regard to the more general matters covered by the Fourteen Points there is little to be said at this stage. Point 1 (no secret treaties) was met in Article 18 of the Treaty. Point 2 (freedom of the seas) had been withdrawn before the armistice and did not come up for discussion. Point 14 (formation of a League of Nations) was carried out by the Treaty, and it should be noticed that from the first Germany's claim to a place in the League as a Great Power was fully recognized. There remain Point 3 (removal of economic barriers) and Point 4 (general disarmament). The Treaty was definitely half-hearted about the former. It did little to reduce existing economic barriers and nothing whatever to stop the building of new economic barriers either by Germany or any of her neighbours. It is worth noticing, however, that the Fourteen Points merely called for the removal *so far as possible* of economic barriers; and in the absence of any statement to the contrary, it was taken as self-evident that each individual State must be the sole judge of what reductions could be effected in its own economic barriers. Moreover, it was officially stated in America that what the President had in mind when he drafted Point 3 was no more than that every member of the League of Nations should automatically grant 'most-favoured-nation' treatment to every other member of the League. We do not need to go in detail into what this means. At the best it could only have meant very little; in fact it meant nothing at all. Point 3 was in fact no more than a pious hope or aspiration. It was drafted and accepted by men who did not understand that no satisfactory peace could be reached which did not face and solve the

---

[1] In addition Germany was, by article 238, charged with the repayment of the war debt incurred by the Belgian Government to the Allies during the period of the war. This was, however, a relatively small item, and the justice of including it in the total has not been seriously disputed.

problems of economic nationalism. And this weakness in the
Fourteen Points was duly carried over into the Treaty.

Point 4, the disarmament point, was in the formal sense
completely met by the Treaty, which not merely reaffirmed the
Allies' intention to disarm 'to the lowest point consistent with
domestic safety', but made arrangements for carrying this resolution into effect by means of the Disarmament Commission of
the League of Nations. The Commission wrestled with the
problem for fourteen weary years, only finally giving up in 1933,
when Hitler cancelled Germany's membership of the League.
The failure of the League's efforts to bring about general disarmament was, of course, primarily due to the short-sightedness
of the victor countries. Not that they failed to disarm in a
sense; many of them—including particularly Britain and the
United States—allowed their armaments to fall well below the
requirements of domestic security. But they did it haphazardly
and, so to speak, by inertia—under pressure from a pacifically
minded and parsimonious public rather than as part of a systematic plan for collective security against a common aggressor;
with the result that when in 1938 the shadow of the Second
World War suddenly darkened the view into the future, they
found themselves utterly and tragically unprepared to meet
the challenge.

But these are matters which concern the events of the twenties
and thirties. We shall have more to say about them in later
chapters. At the moment we are concerned with the specific
and tedious question of the relation between the Fourteen
Points and the Treaty of Versailles. It would not have been
necessary to go into this question at such length had not German
propagandists during the last twenty years disseminated so
successfully—and not merely in Germany—the legend that the
Treaty of Versailles constituted 'the great betrayal' of earlier
Allied promises and assurances. What I have said so far is,
I hope, enough to explode that story for anyone who is willing
to study the facts. The answer to the propagandists is a double
one—though either half would be sufficient taken by itself to
dispose of their case. It is: Firstly, Germany did *not* lay down
her arms because of a promise based on the Fourteen Points;
she laid down her arms from sheer military necessity, knowing
that she must accept any conditions the victors chose to offer;
knowing too that they had explicitly refused to admit the

Fourteen Points among the terms they were prepared to grant for an armistice. And secondly, the Peace of Versailles when it was finally concluded proved, but for one doubtful and, as it turned out, wholly unimportant question about the scale of reparations, to have followed the principles and the specific proposals of the Fourteen Points faithfully and even slavishly; in their weaknesses as well as in their strength.

4.

We have now to deal with the propagandists' second line of attack on the Treaty: that it was *in itself* intolerably harsh and humiliating. To some extent this type of argument conflicts with the arguments we have so far been discussing. For if it be true that the Treaty terms were harsh, then since the Treaty (as we have seen) in almost all respects faithfully copied the Fourteen Points, they too must have been harsh—and what becomes then of the contention that they were put forward as a bait to tempt an unwary Germany by their mildness? But we need not traverse that ground any longer. From now on we are concerned with the Treaty, and the principles it sought to embody, on their merits.

Even here, however, we must delimit the ground rather carefully. It is one thing to discuss whether the Treaty was on its merits just or unjust: it is quite another thing to discuss whether it was wise or foolish. The latter issue can only be decided in the light of subsequent events; it will come up for examination in later chapters of this book. For the moment we are concerned simply with the question of whether Germany at the time could reasonably complain of its terms on the ground of unfairness to her. So circumscribed, the issue can be disposed of without undue trouble. Let us take the arguments of the propagandists on this point one by one.

First the war-guilt clause. Here Germany had, I think, legitimate grounds for protest. Her representative was made to sign a statement that she 'accepted the responsibility', along with the other defeated Powers, for causing all the loss and damage brought about by a war 'imposed upon' the world '*by the aggression of Germany and her allies*' (Art. 231). The intention of this clause was to explain to public opinion in the democratic countries the basis on which reparations were being exacted.

But from the German point of view the sting was in the tail. Many Germans have felt since that in this clause they were branded as war criminals without being given any chance of stating their case. Formally they are right. Propagandists have, of course, greatly exaggerated the extent of the injustice. Clause 231 did not attempt to place the guilt for the First World War exclusively on Germany's shoulders; it specifically included Germany's allies. And the fact is that the immediate responsibility for the outbreak of hostilities in 1914 does rest largely with one of those allies, namely Austria-Hungary. Moreover, Germany herself was certainly not guiltless in the matter. To imply, as the propagandists do, that Germany was wholly innocent—betrayed into a war which was not of her own choosing by her allies—conspired against and wantonly attacked by her foes—is an absurd travesty of the facts. Nevertheless, the Treaty of Versailles was on this point definitely unfair. Whether or not it was true that the war was caused by the aggression of Germany and her allies, it had not been *proved* true by an impartial investigation of the facts at the time when the Treaty was signed.

Secondly, disarmament. Here there can be no possible ground for complaint so far as the Treaty itself is concerned. Germany had been decisively defeated. It was known to the Allies that influential elements in Germany were unwilling to accept the fact of defeat and would take every chance that might come their way to reopen the struggle and try to reverse the decision. The Allies had every right to take steps to prevent that. Their point of view was that Germany must remain disarmed until it became clear that she would not use armaments as a means of starting another world war. Nobody in Germany could justifiably resent such an attitude—least of all those who were in fact planning to do what the Allies proposed to prevent, and for whom 'the war of 1914–18 had never come to an end'.

True, the Allies also affirmed that they intended to reduce their own armaments, and in subsequent years they failed to carry out this intention in the spirit in which it was meant. But there was no suggestion that they would disarm immediately, and it was from the first certain that a period of several years must elapse before Germany could be admitted to a position of equality of rights in this or, for that matter, in any other respect. On the disarmament issue the Treaty must certainly be acquitted of undue harshness, whatever we may think of the wisdom or unwisdom of Allied policy during the ensuing years.

Thirdly, the adjustment of the frontiers of the Reich. Here too the question of 'unfairness' cannot arise. The return of Alsace-Lorraine to France and of northern Schleswig to Denmark represented simply the retrocession of provinces that had been annexed by Germany in the nineteenth century. The territory to be ceded to Poland was determined (as we have seen) strictly in accordance with the principles of nationality and self-determination. Germany's southern frontier remained unchanged—there was no suggestion at the time that the Sudetenlanders should be treated as Germans: they had never belonged to the Reich, and at Versailles neither they themselves nor anybody else demanded that they should now, for the first time in history, acquire German nationality. The Saar area was temporarily detached from Germany for reasons connected with reparations, but there was no question of its cession to France unless its inhabitants so desired. Finally Danzig, which might well have been handed over to Poland, as the latter's natural outlet to the sea, was given a status which enabled it to remain distinctively and essentially German.

The arrangements made at Versailles for settling the territorial problems of the eastern Baltic seaboard were no more than an unsatisfactory makeshift. But that was due to the efforts of the Treaty framers to be *fair* to Germany. Considerations of security and administrative simplicity by themselves would have dictated far harsher terms.

5.

We come now to the colonial question. This is a more complicated issue than those dealt with in the preceding paragraphs, and needs relatively extensive treatment.

The Fourteen Points, as we have seen, laid down that in settling Germany's claims, equal consideration was to be paid to the interests of the native populations and to the 'equitable claims' of their masters.

The interests of the native populations in the former German colonies certainly did not clamour for their restoration. Germany's reputation as a Colonial Power was not good. Stories were plentiful of brutalities practised by German colonists and administrators on the natives of Togoland and Cameroons.

Doubtless many of these were exaggerated—but the main source of them was to be found in the record of Reichstag debates during the pre-war years. It was in fact quite certain that Germany had always regarded her colonies simply as territories for exploitation on the part of the colonists and had felt no responsibility whatever for the interests of the native populations.

To this the propagandists could and unwearyingly did reply that Germany was not alone—was not even the worst offender —in this respect. The Treaty-makers were well aware of this. And when they came to formulate their plans for the future of the former German colonies they worked out a system which, so they hoped, would genuinely safeguard the interests of the native populations in accordance with the spirit of the Fourteen Points. That system—the so-called mandate system—notoriously failed to live up to their expectations. But it was certainly not the farce which the propagandists tried to make it out to be. With the single exception of Japan, every mandatory Power during the decade following upon the conclusion of peace obeyed the conditions of the mandate, in letter and, to a large extent, in spirit. They did not ruthlessly exploit the mandated territories in their own interests; they saw to it that considerable, if inadequate, sums were spent on the education and betterment of the native populations; and if they in some cases drew the mandated territories into closer economic and administrative union with their own adjacent colonies than was contemplated in the Treaty, that was by no means necessarily contrary to the interests of the populations concerned. Not that their actions were inspired by purely unselfish motives. They were not and did not even profess to be. Nor were they always wise or wholly beneficial to the inhabitants. But there is no doubt that on the whole the natives of the former German colonies were in fact better off—and if the intentions of the Treaty-makers had been fully carried out, they would have been far better off—under the mandate system than if they had reverted to German control of the pre-war type.

On balance, therefore, the 'interests of the populations concerned' told in favour of the non-return of the colonies to Germany. What of the 'equitable claims of the Government whose title is to be determined'?

The supporters of the Treaty of Versailles have sometimes tended to interpret this phrase in a way which, in my view, is not legitimate. They have assumed that the 'equitable claims' referred to covered not merely those of Germany but also the rival claims of the Allied Power immediately concerned—Great Britain, South Africa, Japan, or whichever it might happen to be. I do not see how the words can mean that—or rather, I do not think that the Powers concerned could have any 'equitable claim' to the former German colonies at all.[1] But there were other cogent grounds on which the Colonial Powers among the Allies could argue against the return of the German colonies, and the Treaty-makers had every right to take these into account. Point 5 of the Fourteen Points did not profess to give an exhaustive list of the factors to be borne in mind when settling the colonial question; and in any case its application and interpretation had to be carried through in the light of the fundamental principles underlying the Fourteen Points as a whole.

Let us, however, deal first with Germany's 'equitable claim' to her former colonies. The propagandists, incidentally, have from time to time maintained that Germany was never allowed to state her case on the colonial issue. That is only true in the sense that there was never (so far as I know) a formal hearing on the matter before an umpire or arbitrator. But the German representatives were given the opportunity of putting their case forward when the first draft of the Treaty was submitted to them. Their arguments, submitted to the Allies on May 29, 1919, were duly met and answered before the Treaty took its final form. Moreover, it is worth noticing that the language used by the German representatives on this occasion was almost exactly the same as had been used months earlier in the official American Commentary on Point 5. In other words, the basis of the German claim to the return of the colonies was well known to the world long before the question came up for final settlement.

It rested on three points: Germany's right as a great nation to be also a Colonial Power; Germany's economic requirements; and the need of an outlet for her surplus population; to which must be added a fourth unspoken point—the hope on the part of some elements in Germany that colonies could be used to help

[1] By National Socialist standards, of course, the fact that South Africa (for instance) had occupied German South-West Africa by force of arms constituted not merely an equitable claim but an indefeasible right to its permanent retention as an area of private exploitation. But the Allies at Versailles had explicitly renounced the point of view of ownership by conquest.

towards world domination. In order to assess this case properly we must cast a rapid glance at the earlier history of Germany's attitude to her colonies.

Bismarck, as is well known, often declared his opposition, on both economic and strategical grounds, to building up Germany's colonial empire. 'The advantages expected from colonies for the trade and industry of the motherland rest for the most part on illusions', he wrote in 1868. Three years later, when peace was being negotiated with a defeated France, he declared 'I want no colonies. . . . For us colonial undertakings would be like silks and sables in Polish noble families who have no shirts.' And in 1881 he roundly announced that 'so long as I am Reich Chancellor we shall carry out no colonial policy. . . . We must have no vulnerable points in other parts of the world which would serve as booty for France as soon as we were at war with her.'

We need not discuss how far this attitude reflected Bismarck's real convictions or was expressed in his actions as Chancellor. The important thing is that it was not shared by the Kaiser, and the disagreement between the two on this point was one of the main reasons for Bismarck's dismissal. Immediately thereafter Germany's interest in colonies began to take concrete shape. Bismarck's second successor, Hohenlohe, told the Diet in 1894 that 'the maintenance of our colonial empire is a duty to our national honour and a sign of our national prestige'. The Kaiser himself demanded 'a place in the sun' for Germany, and the Agadir crisis in 1911 showed that Germany was entirely ready to go to war, if necessary, for the sake of building up her position as a Colonial Power.

Meanwhile, on the economic side Germany's colonies remained wholly unimportant. At the outbreak of war Germany's imports of raw materials from her colonies amounted to about one two-hundredth of her total raw material imports, and her exports to the colonies were not more significant. Moreover, during the thirty years before the outbreak of the Second World War fewer than 20,000 Germans had emigrated to the colonial empire.

Clearly, therefore, the argument from prestige—as strengthened in some people's minds by the belief in colonies as a stepping-stone to world empire—was the driving force behind the German demand for colonies in the post-war years. It was

not an argument which was likely to impress the Allies, or for
that matter the world as a whole, however passionately it was
felt by Germans. To the latter the disappearance of the German
colonial empire was a symbol of defeat which they learnt to
resent as the years passed; for the Allies Germany's defeat was
merely a fact, and if the loss of colonies was unwelcome to many
Germans simply on prestige grounds, that certainly could not
be held to constitute an 'equitable claim' for their return.

Moreover, on the economic issue a further point must be
borne in mind. Germany might have argued that the economic
insignificance of the colonial empire in the past was no evidence
whatever of its continuing economic insignificance in years to
come. In the light of subsequent events this contention looks
far from unplausible. If Germany had been a Colonial Power
during the National Socialist period, there is no doubt whatever
that the colonial areas would have been drawn into the Four
Years Plan, their resources would have been developed and
exploited to the utmost in the interests of autarky, and in due
course both the size of the German population in the colonial
territories and the volume of trade between them and the
mother country would have expanded to substantial propor-
tions.[1] If all this could have been foreseen in 1919 Germany's
case for the return of her colonies on economic grounds would
have been more forceful—though it would also have evoked
corresponding counter-arguments on behalf of the other world
Powers—and of the native populations—and the final decision
on the issue would not have been reversed!

At the time, however, this case was not put forward; it hardly
could have been with any degree of conviction. And on the
Allied side it was pointed out that to deprive Germany of
colonies as spheres of control did not involve cutting her off
from access to their natural resources. The international scene
was not darkened in 1919 with policies of autarky and foreign
exchange restrictions; the world's greatest Colonial Power,
Great Britain, still scrupulously adhered to her 'open-door'
policy and allowed no discrimination between British and non-
British traders in the colonial markets; it was clearly understood
that the same policy should be followed in the new mandated
territories. Under these circumstances, and in view of the
economic unimportance of the German colonies in the past, it

[1] See further on this Chapter VI, pp. 156 ff., esp. 158-9.

was not plausible to argue that their non-return would be a source of grave loss to Germany's economic well-being.

But if it did not occur to the Treaty-makers that the colonial empire might become *economically* important to Germany in the post-war years, they were well aware of its potential *military* value. The case put forward by the other Colonial Powers—and not by them alone—against meeting Germany's claim rested on precisely this ground. In the First World War the German colonies had been potent sources of trouble to the Allied Powers, until they were one by one conquered: in a Second World War their potentialities would doubtless have been greatly extended—for example by the establishment in them of well-equipped U-boat bases and airfields. The threat to Allied security was obvious. And there can be no doubt that it was this consideration, more than anything else, which settled that the colonies were not to be returned to Germany.

Before any German denounces this decision as unjust, let him reflect whether the Allied fears which gave rise to it were well founded or not.[1]

6.

Finally, the reparations problem. Once again, we are not concerned with the wisdom of what was decided at Versailles nor with what was actually done during subsequent years, but merely with the question whether the reparations clauses of the Treaty were in any reasonable sense 'unjust' or unduly harsh to Germany.

There was clearly nothing unjust in the *principle* of exacting reparations. That had been accepted as a usage of war-making for centuries. Indeed it was the time-honoured practice of all victorious nations to extract from their defeated opponents not merely 'reparation' for damage they had themselves suffered but indemnities and tributes. This practice was of course loyally adhered to by Germany after wars in which she was victorious. For example in the peace settlement with France in 1871 and in the Treaty of Brest-Litovsk. In neither case was there any question of reparations for damage to German civilians or their property, because the fighting had taken place exclusively on non-German soil. Nevertheless, in 1871 Bismarck presented France with a bill amounting to twice Germany's total war

---

[1] For more on the colonial question see below, pp. 111 ff., 156 ff.

costs. And at Brest-Litovsk the Russians were ordered to pay Germany a total of six milliard gold marks in money, securities, and goods. From this point of view the Treaty of Versailles marked a big advance in leniency towards the defeated side.

What, then, of the *amount* of reparations demanded? The Treaty of Versailles did not specify a figure, leaving it for investigation and settlement by a specially appointed Reparation Commission. The bill when it was presented was large. It was bound to be; for the amount of damage inflicted by the German Army on civilian property was also large. Particularly during their last retreat, in the autumn of 1918, they had systematically destroyed villages, slaughtered cattle, dismantled factories, put coal-mines out of order, removed stocks and equipment. This was done by the deliberate orders of the High Command. It was a last desperate effort to postpone defeat by delaying the Allied advance. And apart from this, they had throughout the war been prepared to carry out savage reprisals against French and Belgian civilians—or against whole communities—for failure to co-operate in the German war effort against their own countries. To all of which must be added the destruction of merchant shipping in the U-boat war. Even if the Reparations Bill had not included the item for pensions and separation allowances—for which there is quite a reasonable case to be made out on its merits but which we have already condemned as being a departure from the intention of the Fourteen Points— even without that item the total bill for damage would have amounted to many milliards of marks.

Now the Allies had in principle every right to work out the total amount of damage suffered by their civilians at Germany's hands and to regard that as the total sum due in reparation. That can only be denied by some one who disputes the right of a victor to call upon his defeated enemies to make good the damage he has suffered during the struggle; and Germans are in no position to adopt such a standpoint in view of Germany's own record in this matter. But what if the debtor is unable to pay the whole sum demanded? Where those concerned are individuals the universal practice is to call upon the debtor to pay all that he reasonably can; and the creditor has willy-nilly to treat the deficit as an irrecoverable loss. This was precisely the point of view adopted by the Treaty-makers at Versailles. In Article 232 they specifically expressed their recognition that 'the resources of Germany are not adequate ... to make complete reparation for all loss and damage' suffered by the Allied and Associated Governments and their nationals. And therefore the question to be settled by the Reparation Commission was not 'How much does Germany owe?', but rather 'How much can Germany pay?'

The figure eventually arrived at by the Reparation Commission, and communicated on May 5, 1921, to the German Government, was 132 milliard gold marks. Payment was to be spread over forty-two years, and on the basis of 5 per cent. interest on the unpaid portion of the total the annual sum due worked out at an average of about 7 milliard gold marks. Germany was therefore to pay reparations at the rate of some 2 marks per week per head of the population.

Was this demand reasonable or unreasonable?

From a practical point of view it was unreasonable. That is to say, it represented more than could be *transferred* from Germany to the Allied States without hopelessly upsetting the structure of international trade and finance. This is a matter to which we shall come back in the next chapter. Here, too, the Treaty-makers showed their failure to understand the economic side of the problems confronting them.

But is there any case for saying that it was unreasonable from the point of view of the German payers? Germany was to be asked to pay an amount equivalent, very roughly, to something of the order of 10 per cent. of what might be expected to be her total national income once normal peace-time conditions had been restored. That represented a heavy burden; the standard of living of the German people would be that much lower than it would have been. But the bill to be paid was entirely in respect of damage suffered and expenses incurred by the governments and peoples of the victors. If Germany did not pay it, then the Allies would have to; they, the victors, would have a heavier economic burden to bear than Germany, their defeated enemy—for once again let us remember that *German* civilian property was hardly touched by the ravages of the First World War.

Moreover, 2 marks per head per week, though heavy, was certainly not a *crushing* burden for a people of Germany's economic standing. Let us not forget that during the first six and a half years of the National Socialist era, as Hitler boasted at the outbreak of the Second World War, Germany spent in all 90 milliard marks on armaments—at least 4 marks per head per week; almost a quarter of the German national income. Let us not forget, too, that between the summer of 1940 and the end of 1943 Germany collected 36 milliard marks from France— fully two and a half times as heavy a burden per head as the Allies ever sought to impose on Germany after the First World War.

No, whatever we may think of the *wisdom*, from the point of view of practicability and economic consequences, of the reparations demands made upon Germany in the peace settlement, the contention that they represented a monstrous *injustice* to the defeated Powers will not stand up to even the most perfunctory analysis.

7.

It appears, then, that the Treaty of Versailles was in no sense the unjust and cynical imposition that the propagandists alleged it to have been. It neither departed from the principles of the Fourteen Points in any particular of major importance, nor was it unjust on its merits, except in so far as it pinned a share of the responsibility for the war on to Germany without submitting the whole question of war guilt to a thorough and impartial analysis.

And yet throughout the twenties the propagandists vented the whole of their spleen on this painstaking document, and by the middle of the thirties practically every ordinary German had become convinced that the Treaty of Versailles was a scandal and an imposition, a travesty of justice, a deliberate attempt to humiliate and injure the innocent German people. How are we to account for so wild an error?

In the case of the nationalist elements among the German ruling caste the explanation is partly no doubt to be found in the words of Prince Max of Baden, quoted in Chapter I. These people had seen in the Fourteen Points a bargaining counter which 'a skilful German diplomacy might turn to Germany's advantage at the conference table'. They were disappointed in their hopes. The Treaty did not give them all the opportunities they had looked for. It killed the prospects of an early resumption of the war under conditions reasonably favourable to Germany. If they were to carry out their plans at all they must work slowly and secretly and not hope for results for many years to come. That is what they did—as we shall see in the next chapter. But in the meantime it was natural for them to vent their indignation on the Treaty, the instrument of their disappointment, and to tell themselves that because it had foiled their plans therefore it was unjust and 'unfair'.

But so far as the German people as a whole is concerned a different sort of explanation must be found.

The explanation, I believe, is twofold.

First, the pride of Germany was mortally hurt by the fact of defeat in a major war. The thought of that defeat was almost intolerable; and by a natural instinct of emotional self-protection the average German cast about to find a way of escaping from admitting the thought of it into his conscious mind. One way of achieving that was to deny that Germany ever had been defeated. There lay the origin of the stab-in-the-back legend and of the readiness of many personally brave and decent Germans to believe it notwithstanding the shocking slur they cast on their own honour in so doing. The other way was to transfer the feeling of humiliation from the defeat itself to the Treaty which symbolized it. If one could tell oneself that the *Treaty* was unjust, wicked, a deliberate humiliation of Germany on the part of arrogant foreign Powers—why, then it might be possible to push into the background of one's mind the *real* source of the feeling of humiliation—the fact that Germany had been soundly and decisively beaten in war. One could accuse one's enemies of brutality instead of accusing oneself of failure.

Hence when the propagandists came to spread abroad the legend of the Fourteen Points and the Treaty they found the ground well prepared. Propaganda by itself could not have achieved the result. It had to appeal to feelings already present in its audience. The plain truth is that on this point the ordinary German *wanted* to believe the propagandists, and he lent an uncritical ear to their arguments. Had he been less anxious to be persuaded, had he been prepared to study and understand the facts of the case realistically, even when they were painful to him, the history of the last twelve years might have been much less disastrous both for himself and for the world as a whole.

As it was, the two legends of the stab in the back and the great betrayal directly supported and strengthened one another. If the Treaty was a great betrayal, then that implied that better things had been promised before the war was over; how natural,

then, to conclude that somehow the prospect of these better
things had played a part in deciding Germany to lay down her
arms, and from that to go on and say that Germany was tricked
and betrayed into surrender and never beaten in the military
sense at all. On the other hand, if one had persuaded oneself
that Germany was not beaten, then the fact that the Treaty was
based on the assumption that Germany *was* beaten became an
added source of resentment and protest against its contents.
Why the deep indignation at the provisions for revising the
frontiers of the Reich; for reparations (miscalled tribute by
the propagandists); for unilateral disarmament; for placing the
colonies under international control? Not because they broke
any natural canons of justice or fair dealing, nor because they
contravened previously announced pledges, for they did neither;
but simply and utterly because they confirmed and symbolized
the position of Germany as a defeated nation. Thus just because
the fact of defeat was too painful to be admitted, it became not
merely a right but a positive duty to resent and hate the Treaty
as the instrument whereby that intolerable fact was displayed
to view. Let me ask any German who in his time has believed
in the legend of the great betrayal: is it not the case that the
source of his indignation with the Treaty of Versailles was, with
the single exception of the eight words relating to war guilt,
due to his own attempts to deny to himself that Germany was
in 1919 a defeated nation?

The second reason for the success of the Versailles legend is
this. For the first time in history—if we except the Treaty
between Great Britain and South Africa at the end of the Boer
War—an attempt was avowedly made in 1919 by the victors in
a war to build a peace based not on force but on right. The
attempt was not very successful. The victors made many and
grave mistakes, for which they may rightly be censured. But
these mistakes were almost entirely caused by ignorance—by
an oversimplification of the problem at issue, by blind adherence
to an inadequate concept of nationality and national self-determination, by a total failure to understand the importance of the
economic factors involved. They were not due either to malice
against their defeated enemies nor to any desire to depart from
the principles they had set up for themselves. As President
Wilson said on September 27, 1918, 'The impartial justice
meted out must involve no discrimination between those to

whom we wish to be just and those to whom we do not wish to be just.' To this guiding principle the Allies attempted to conform throughout the work of framing the Treaty. They did not like the Germans, the bitterness of the war was still upon them, but they nevertheless tried to be just.

And precisely because they made this effort they rendered themselves vulnerable to the shafts of the propagandists. These could point to the many hardships involved in the Treaty, they could deliberately confuse hardship with injustice—and in this way they forged a powerful weapon for arousing resentment against the Treaty and its authors among their readily persuadable audience; for a supposed injustice always seems harder to bear if the author of it claims to be acting in the name of justice. Hence the Treaty of Versailles aggravated the prejudice that Germany was bound to feel against it in any case by the very fact that it set itself so high a standard.

Whether these explanations of the success of the Versailles legend will be accepted by Germans to-day I do not know. But the fact remains, and, I submit, has been abundantly proved in the preceding pages, that the Peace of Versailles, setting out to be both a good and a just peace, failed, through the ignorance and short-sightedness of its authors, to be good, but succeeded triumphantly in the lesser task of being just.

IV

FROM THE TREATY TO THE SEIZURE OF POWER

I.

THE weaknesses in the Versailles settlement soon began to show themselves. The first blow—it was a crushing one—was struck when the American Senate refused to ratify the Treaty. The reason for this was largely a matter of internal American politics. Presidential and Congressional elections had been fought, and won, on the platform of opposition to Wilson and all that he stood for. They expressed the determination of the United States to dissociate itself from Allied efforts to build up a new world order. America retired into a shell of isolationism, from which it did not fully emerge until after the election of Roosevelt as President in 1932.

The consequences of this disaster were to make themselves felt in all parts of the world and in all sectors of the international problem. The United States refused to take any part in the administration of the former German colonies, and therefore the whole mandate system became an object of suspicion; for America was the one country which was universally regarded as being above reproach in the matter of colonial imperialism. And at the same time isolationism brought with it a policy of high tariffs, which, apart from its generally depressing effect on international economic relations and its encouragement to other nations to follow and surpass the American example, had the immediate consequence of making the settlement of large-scale international debts completely impossible, as we shall see in a moment. The League of Nations itself was to a considerable extent discredited from the outset: popular opinion in the democratic countries regarded it either as a piece of pious idealism carrying no prospect of immediate usefulness—e.g. in Great Britain—or else as a mere tool for furthering a negative and self-regarding policy of military security—e.g. in France. We cannot blame France for taking this attitude. The fault lay with her allies. Rightly or wrongly they had rejected her demand for the permanent occupation of the left bank of the Rhine, offering her in return a joint Anglo-American guarantee of her eastern frontier in case of any act of German aggression.

America had now repudiated this guarantee. Britain felt that in consequence she too was released from her obligation. France was thus left to fend for herself. On the one hand deserted by the other Great Powers (for Russia had disappeared for the time being from the political scene and Italy was beginning to think along her own lines—lines not friendly towards France); on the other hand, faced by a Germany of whose future intentions she had every reason to feel nervous; she took the only policy open to her—the maintenance of her own defences and the organization of alliances and agreements with the smaller States of central and eastern Europe who felt themselves similarly threatened.

Under these circumstances the attempt to carry out the policy of general disarmament as envisaged in the Peace Treaty was bound to fail. It is to the credit of the League of Nations that it tried so hard and so long to devise a way of carrying out that policy. It was an impossible task. France and her allies would not disarm except within the framework of a watertight system of collective security ensuring common action against an aggressor. But America had washed her hands of Europe and would have nothing to do with any joint plans for preserving the peace. Britain too turned France down. For a number of reasons. Partly from laziness: the British people were tired of war, wanted a quiet life, did not relish the thought of taking on world commitments for the future. Partly from pessimism arising out of the withdrawal of America; for many people in England even at that time recognized that the hope of world peace must in the end depend on co-operation between the English-speaking peoples. Partly from a growing feeling of friendship towards Germany and a desire to let bygones be bygones: the average Englishman neither understood nor sympathized with French fears of her eastern neighbour—largely perhaps because he had not had personal experience of a German military occupation. And partly from the growth of an 'isolationist' feeling, comparable with, though far less pervasive than, the isolationism of the United States; the feeling, namely, that Britain's best prospects for peace and prosperity lay in turning her back on Europe and devoting herself to her overseas possessions and to the commonwealth of the Self-governing Dominions. It was a foolish idea this—that in an aeroplane age the British Isles could, if they chose, dissociate themselves from the Continent of Europe and its problems. Nor was it shared by everybody in Britain, nor accepted whole-heartedly by any except a handful of fanatical imperialists. But it sufficed to determine the British attitude towards the European situation; an attitude of co-operating with France and the other States of Europe only to that minimum extent which might seem inescapable in order to avoid the threat of a second world war.

This divergence between the attitude of Britain and of France received its definitive expression in the winter of 1922–3. France and the other Allies had all been dissatisfied with the way in which Germany, in their view, was failing to carry out the letter and still more the spirit of the Peace Treaty. Reparations payments had not been up to the standard demanded; Germany had not completed her own disarmament to their satisfaction; Germany had taken no steps to bring her war criminals to trial. France and Belgium took the view that the time had come to apply sanctions. They therefore proposed to extend the area of occupation to the Ruhr valley.

Now there is no doubt that Germany had been guilty of these breaches of the Treaty—a fact which will neither surprise nor shock any German who regards the peace settlement as an imposition which she was right in evading and nullifying to the best of her ability. Nor is there any doubt that in the light of these breaches the Allies were entitled under the terms of the Treaty to take punitive action—though the legality of the particular action taken is a matter on which there was room for much argument. But the occupation of the Ruhr was bound to cause resentment in Germany and could only retard the process of pacification for which Britain hoped. Therefore the British Government opposed the step and in the end France carried it out by herself. The British objection, it should be stressed, was *not* based on a feeling of friendship towards Germany, though admittedly the bitterness of the war years had by then been largely forgotten by British—unlike French—public opinion. What concerned the British Government and people was simply and solely whether the measure proposed would help towards achieving the 'quiet life' which was all that Britain asked for. But the result of the Ruhr occupation was to increase in France the feeling that she was being let down by her allies and in Britain the feeling that France was being unnecessarily harsh if not actually unjust to her former enemy. A sense of sympathy for Germany was undoubtedly kindled in many Englishmen by that episode, as also was a sense of estrangement from France.[1]

In this way the coalition of the victorious Powers, which was to have been the guarantee of an enduring peace and the cornerstone of a new world order, crumbled away in mutual suspicion and friction and disunity.

2.

In the economic field the results of the new attitude of the English-speaking world were no less devastating. The financial situation was exacerbated beyond belief. For the United States, not being concerned in the collection of reparations, became all the more resolute on the question of her own war debts and made it clear that she expected that her former comrades in arms should pay in full the sums that she had lent them during the course of the war. This was, of course, an entirely intelligible standpoint on the assumption, then almost universally accepted in the United States, that the war was a purely European affair and the war debts a strictly business proposition. But it inevitably increased the friction between the victor Powers. And it also made it certain that Britain and France would insist upon the exaction of reparations from Germany to the full extent of her capacity to pay them. Britain's policy on this point was clear. She had been a net creditor in the war operations, that is to say, she had lent more to the other Allies than she had borrowed from America. It was certain that her debtors would not be in a position to pay all they owed. Therefore she must make up the deficit by seeing to it that Germany met her obligations. On the other hand, it was to Britain's interest as the leading participator in world trade that international economic relations should return to a normal peace-time basis as completely and as quickly as possible. From the British point of view, therefore, the ideal thing would have been the cancellation of all war debts and a substantial scaling-down of reparations. But such a policy would have been anathema to the United States. And therefore, as a second best, Britain adopted and announced the principle that she would demand as much from

[1] The end of the Ruhr occupation 2½ years later, in August 1925, was the direct result of British pressure on France. It was the immediate prelude to the signing of the Locarno Treaty, in which the British standpoint as to the best way of handling the German problem received its fullest expression. See below on this, p. 84.

her debtors as she owed to the United States—as much but no more. France meanwhile badly needed reparations as a means as much of paying her debts to Britain and America as of balancing her own budget. In view of all this, and in the embittered atmosphere of the post-war years, there was no chance that the reparations question would be given the objective consideration that it required. The question asked was always: How can we get from Germany the money which she can justly be called upon to pay, and which we badly need? The real issue—how the huge unilateral payments involved in the settlement of reparations and war debts could be effected without throwing the whole mechanism of international trade into chaos —was never squarely faced, except in the unavailing writings of a few economists.[1]

Nor was this all. Isolationism in America and Empire-mindedness in Great Britain brought economic nationalism in their train. The United States again gave the lead with the introduction in 1922 of a new and high scale of tariffs against industrial imports from the outside world. Britain followed suit with a policy of 'Imperial Preferences', which were intended to encourage trade within the Empire but in fact merely discouraged trade with other countries and—worse still—entailed the abandonment of the open-door policy with regard to the British colonies. Meanwhile the Self-governing Dominions were busily engaged in developing their own industrial resources and for this purpose began to step up their tariffs—not merely against the outside world but also against one another and the mother country; so that in effect there came to be one (comparatively low) tariff wall round the British Commonwealth as a whole, and in addition a series of further walls isolating its separate component parts. The path of economic nationalism was also, of course, followed—with perhaps better excuse—by the new or reconstructed States of central and eastern Europe. They, too, walled themselves round with tariffs against the outside world. They had, of course, every right to do so. It had not occurred to the Treaty-makers to limit their economic sovereignty; they were proudly conscious of their new nationhood and determined to express their economic independence

[1] Particularly, of course, J. M. Keynes (now Lord Keynes), whose books *The Economic Consequences of the Peace* and *A Revision of the Treaty* aroused world-wide interest but had little effect on contemporary international policy.

by building up their own budding industries. On all sides, therefore, the trend was away from the free international exchange of goods which might have contributed so much, had it been achieved, towards the pacification and restoration of the war-scarred world.

We must not, indeed, exaggerate the harm done to the international situation by the growth of tariffs during the twenties. They undoubtedly meant economic loss and an unnecessarily low standard of living throughout the whole world, and they also contributed, at least indirectly, to the severity of the great depression in the early thirties. But as such they were no more than a continuance of the pre-war approach to international economic relations, and there was at the time no reason to see in them a source of political instability or war. Still less were they in any sense directed specifically against *Germany*; they were inspired rather by a semi-conscious distrust of foreigners in general. Nor was Germany the chief sufferer from them; that melancholy honour must undoubtedly be ascribed to Great Britain, which depended more than any other country in the world upon international trade for its own prosperity and for which the twenties brought nothing but a long and weary struggle against endemic industrial depression. Germany's sufferings—from *this* cause—were relatively light, and there is of course no truth whatever in the picture later drawn by the propagandists of her being deliberately 'cut off' from her overseas sources of supplies.[1]

But in one respect the growth of economic nationalism in this period did have a decisive influence on the course of world events. It made the payment of reparations (and, as it turned out in the end, of war debts) virtually impossible. The only way whereby reparation payments could be effected was by the exports of *goods* from the paying country to the receiving country. That was a simple and inescapable economic fact—for Germany had little gold or foreign investments and she could only acquire foreign exchange for paying her creditors by selling to the outside world the products and services of her citizens' labour. The payment of reparations on the scale envisaged by the peace settlement would thus have entailed an enormous increase in Germany's exports—an increase sufficient to make her the main industrial exporting country in the world. But the

[1] See below, Chapter V, pp. 94 ff.

world did not want Germany's—or anyone else's—exports. America in particular had shown that she was not prepared to contemplate a huge increase in industrial imports and would raise and re-raise her tariffs to any extent necessary for preventing such an increase. Other receiving countries adopted a similar if not so extreme standpoint. And it was therefore quite certain, long before the end of the twenties, that the reparations arrangements would break down; they *could* not be successful so long as the Western Powers maintained their policy of (so to speak) demanding reparations with one hand while refusing to accept them with the other.

Public and governmental opinion was, however, slow to recognize this simple and indisputable economic fact; largely because it was for many years masked by another phenomenon which could not have been anticipated beforehand. From 1924 until the middle of 1930 foreign money streamed into Germany in a fantastic volume. During those five and a half years it is estimated that Germany's foreign debt went up by more than 30 milliard marks. A small proportion of this total was directly concerned with facilitating the payment of reparations—for the Dawes Plan, while not scaling down the total reparations claim, had recognized the need for some interim support to Germany's finances, and under its auspices the creditor States advanced some 800 million marks to the German Government. But the whole of the rest—more than 97 per cent. of the total—represented private transactions between investors abroad and borrowers (or sellers) inside Germany. The transactions took all possible forms: the purchase of German industrial shares and real estate, long- and short-term bond issues, bankers' acceptances, the placing of money at call. The borrowers in Germany included states and municipalities, public utilities, banks, industrial and commercial concerns, even churches and charities. There is no doubt that they contributed greatly to improving Germany's industrial capacity and the standard of life of the German people.

Moreover, they did more than that: they offset, and indeed far more than offset, Germany's reparations payments. Between the end of the war and the middle of 1930 something over 10 milliard marks represented the sum total of reparations delivered in cash by Germany to the victor Powers. This sum was thus covered *three times over* by the inflow of cash from these same Powers and from neutral countries like Holland and Switzerland in the form of commercial loans and credits. Small wonder, then, that for the time being there was no difficulty about the extra German exports needed to look after reparations payments. During the twenties Germany was actually *importing* substantially more in real goods than she was exporting.

Some people have deduced from this that Germany in effect paid no reparations at all but on the contrary received during the eleven years after the peace settlement a substantial net gift from her former enemies. But that does not follow from these two figures. For, on the one hand, in assessing Germany's total reparations performance it is proper and necessary to add two further items to the cash payments: first Germany's foreign investments and property which were requisitioned under the Treaty, and secondly deliveries in kind such as deliveries of coal and of merchant shipping. It is unfortunately quite impossible to estimate the value of these two sets of items even approximately, but they may well between them have amounted to almost 30 milliard marks. And, on the other hand, the figure of the foreign loans to Germany outstanding in the middle of 1930 must be supplemented by the loans and investments by foreigners effected before and during the inflation period. It is estimated that as a result of the inflation Germany's foreign creditors lost assets to the value of 11 milliard gold marks—in the form of worthless mortgages, bonds, bank notes, and so on.[1]

Thus it may be that in a final balance between Germany's *total* out-payments on account of reparations and her *total* receipts from foreign loans and investments up to the summer of 1930, it would emerge that the two were of more or less the same order of magnitude. Certainly there can be no question of a heavy excess of the former. And we may therefore take it that *in fact* Germany paid no reparations at all during these eleven years and may even have received a net 'gift' from the outside world.

This was, of course, very far from representing the intentions of the creditor nations. In making these huge loans they were thinking of their own commercial interests and prospects. They believed Germany to be a good investment, they over-estimated her financial soundness once the inflation had been overcome,

---

[1] It should be emphasized that the figures in this paragraph are only of the nature of rough approximations. For a number of reasons accuracy in these matters is impossible.

they relied upon her good faith. Moreover, for various reasons into which we need not enter, liquid capital was more than abundant during the second half of the twenties. Investors, particularly in the United States, were eagerly searching for outlets for their funds. And Germany seemed to offer an excellent opportunity for the profitable use of their capital. Nobody will at the present day feel disposed to sympathize with them on account of their heavy losses.[1]

Nevertheless, even from the German point of view, the situation soon became extremely unhealthy. In the first place, the accumulation of a heavy load of commercial debt on top of the reparations obligations meant that in the future, as interest on that debt became due, the problem of achieving a sufficient excess of exports over imports would become all the more acute. In other words, the inflow of foreign capital between 1924 and the summer of 1930 had concealed the difficulty of combining reparations demands with a policy of high tariffs, and had postponed the need for finding a solution; but so far from itself providing such a solution, it had merely made the problem itself more acute. And secondly, a substantial proportion of the loans—nearly half the total—were of a short-term nature. These represented an obvious source of instability; they meant that if Germany's creditors decided to call them back, Germany's position would be seriously compromised.

For both these reasons the German Government, under

[1] To complete the balance sheet of reparations and foreign loans up to the beginning of 1933 it should be added that (a) from the middle of 1930 till the summer of 1931 Germany paid a further 2 milliard marks in reparations—thereafter reparations payments stopped altogether; (b) between the middle of 1930 and the end of 1932 foreign capital was withdrawn from Germany to the extent of perhaps 6 milliard marks. On the assumption, therefore (which, as we have seen, is extremely rough and ready), that in the middle of 1930 Germany had received in private and governmental loans approximately the same amount as she had paid out in reparations, the position when Hitler came to power was that Germany had in the 13½ years of the Weimar Republic paid out a net 8 milliard marks. She was, however, still liable in respect of the outstanding private debts and foreign investments, totalling more than 20 milliard marks. During the following 6½ years the total fell by a further 10 milliards or so—partly owing to the efforts of Germany's creditors to retrieve their capital and of emigrants to transfer resources abroad (in spite of the exchange restrictions, on which see below, pp. 94 ff.), but chiefly because of the devaluation of sterling and other currencies, which lowered the mark value of most of Germany's foreign debts and facilitated the repurchase of foreign bonds. These in any case stood at a low price in the world stock exchanges owing to the German failure to transfer interest payments on them.

pressure from the Agent General for Reparations, took steps to
control and even discourage foreign borrowing on the part of
German States and municipalities. But their efforts were half-
hearted in themselves and met with opposition and obstruction
from the bodies concerned. The latter wished to improve their
tramways, their electricity works and so on, and if that could
be done on foreign capital then so much the better. And the
stream of foreign capital flowed into Germany with undimi-
nished volume.

Meanwhile the Allies had at last realized that the transfer of
reparations payments amounting to 7 or 8 milliard marks a year
was liable to cause difficulties for Germany's foreign exchanges
and indeed for the whole structure of international trade. During 1929 they worked out, in conjunction with the German
authorities, a new series of arrangements, subsequently known
as the Young Plan, the effect of which was to cut down Germany's reparations obligations by more than a half.

But it was too late. Scarcely had the Young Plan been ratified
when the economic storm broke. In October 1929 there was a
sharp slump in the New York stock exchange. American investors suddenly became nervous about their foreign loans,
American banks were faced with abnormal demands for cash at
home and covered themselves by cutting down on their foreign
credits, the flow of funds to Germany began to dry up and by
the summer of 1930 had tapered off into a net withdrawal, which
became heavier the more Germany's creditors realized the un-
soundness of her financial position. Various stopgap measures
were introduced to stabilize the situation, but the flight of
foreign capital from Germany continued. In the spring of 1931
came the failure of a big Austrian bank, followed in the summer
by the failure of a still bigger German bank. Two months later
Great Britain, for all her financial strength, found herself faced
with a flight of capital across the Atlantic larger than her resources could stand, and was forced off the gold standard.

All this completely transformed the world financial picture.

In the first place it meant the end of reparations. In the
summer of 1931 the American President proposed a year's
moratorium on all reparations and war debts payments. This
was accepted by the other Allies—gladly by Great Britain,
reluctantly by France.[1]

[1] In both countries it was realized that reparations payments, once stopped,

Secondly, in August a conference of international bankers agreed to an international financial 'standstill', i.e. to the prolongation of existing short-term loans to Germany for a period of at least six months. Thus was initiated the era of 'frozen' credits and 'blocked' accounts. The intention was, of course, merely to tide over the existing crisis and to help Germany to recover her financial stability. But the German authorities saw in it a superb new weapon for defaulting on foreign debts, for tightening their control over Germany's own economic system, and, not least, for increasing German bargaining power in trade dealings with other countries. The system of foreign exchange restrictions had come to stay, as an integral part of the National Socialist financial system.[1]

That, then, is the story of Allied policy towards Germany during the thirteen and a half years between the Peace of Versailles and the National Socialists' seizure of power. It is largely a story of ignorance, short-sightedness, and inertia; of failure to understand the political and economic issues involved, of failure to remain united, above all, of failure to realize the dangers ahead. France at least, as we have seen, did realize these dangers; but she was unable to convince her former Allies of their reality and by herself she was powerless to ward them off.

'Si les Français avaient pu, si les autres avaient su !'

3.

For the danger was real and urgent. In order to assess it we must study the history of these years from the German side.

We have already noted that from the first the German authorities evaded the obligations imposed upon them by the Treaty so far as they could and dared. Their attitude was due not merely to a human and understandable desire to get the better of the victors—a point of view which was undoubtedly shared by the vast mass of the German people—it was also due to a deliberate intention of doing everything possible to prepare for a Second World War. Only a minority of the people wanted and were prepared to work for that. The great majority of Germans were as anxious as were the British to forget the past and settle down

were not likely to be resumed; and this was in the interest of the British policy, but not of the French, so long as it was accompanied by the cancellation of inter-Allied war debts.
  [1] See further below, pp. 94 ff.

to a life of peace and international co-operation. But the minority was influential. It included the officers of the former General Staff, who remained in control of Germany's military affairs after the war was over; high executives of the Ministries and Government Departments; judges of the criminal and civil courts; and above all it included the big industrialists of the west and the big landowners of the east. Some members of the Government supported, or at least connived at, their activities; those who did not were simply kept in ignorance of what was going on. Thus from the very beginning was launched a huge conspiracy for recreating Germany's war potential; a conspiracy directed not merely against the Allies but also against the German people itself.

There is no need to trace its course in detail, for the facts are by this time public property, having been openly admitted by the leaders of the Third Reich, once they had achieved their object in the summer of 1939. All we need do is to give some indication of its range and thoroughness.[1]

The most vital task was to maintain the German Army in existence, not simply as the militia envisaged by the Treaty of Versailles, but as a potential striking force. This task involved several elements.

First it involved retaining in military service any ex-soldiers or ex-officers who were willing to help. These were at first organized in a series of scattered 'Free Corps', which, under various innocent-sounding titles and in the guise of sports associations, travellers' clubs, or even commercial enterprises, carried on a kind of gangster existence interspersed with regular military training. Later they came more and more under central direction and formed the 'Black Militia', as it was called. This was not a large body numerically; it probably never totalled more than thirty thousand men. But these men were trained and organized to be the cadre of the German Army of the future; they were to provide the framework of militarist experience and ideology into which millions of German youths and men could be fitted when the time was ripe for coming out into the open. When Hitler announced the introduction of general conscription he had in the corps of professional soldiers of the Black Militia the machinery for translating this decision into imme-

[1] An excellent résumé of the problems of secret rearmament is to be found in the official German *Yearbook of the German Army*, 1941, p. 58.

diate and effective action; and that machinery had been created more than ten years before he came to power.

Secondly, the General Staff itself had to be kept in being. Formally it was disbanded under the terms of the peace settlement. But Germany was still entitled to have a Defence (or Militia) Ministry. And in that Ministry there was created a 'General Troops Office'. Nobody knew officially what this section was supposed to do—but three weeks after the signing of the Treaty one of the two or three oldest staff officers of the German Army, General von Seeckt, became its Director, and its members for several years were also primarily recruited from the former General Staff. In this way the General Staff survived, disguised as a Government Department. But its activities were cramped by financial difficulties—its expenditure had to be fitted into the limited budget of the Defence Ministry, and this soon ceased to be adequate. Therefore in 1926 a new method was adopted. General von Schleicher founded a business concern called the 'German Military Policy and Military Sciences Company'. This was in form an ordinary commercial enterprise and what it did was no formal concern of the Allies. Its finances were obtained from many hundred industrial firms, all of them headed by men of nationalist leanings, all of them likely to benefit by huge contracts if Germany ever started to rearm. By means of this device the General Staff was not merely relieved of financial stringency, it was also given an appearance of legality; for as the Defence Minister, Otto Gessler, had remarked in 1925, 'There is no clause in the Peace Treaty which forbids us to reconstitute the General Staff in the form of a corporation with limited liability'.

And thirdly, the black army had to be provided with weapons. In the early days this was done by hiding and preserving equipment and arms which had survived from the war and which, according to the Treaty, were due for destruction. The Allies had established a Military Control Commission to supervise this work. Its task was to trace and frustrate German attempts—which the Allies knew of course would be made—to prevent the destruction of existing armaments or to embark on the construction of new armaments. The Free Corps, and later the Black Militia, set themselves to the task of outwitting the Allied Commission. Many vivid stories are told of how they succeeded in concealing guns and tanks and even big artillery from the French and British inspectors. Thanks to their efforts Germany could truthfully say that in spite of the Peace Treaty she had never really been disarmed.

At the same time every effort was made to carry on with the production of new weapons and equipment. In so far as these were obviously and exclusively military in character they had either to conform to the modest limits imposed upon armaments construction by the Treaty, or else to be carried out in conditions of the strictest secrecy. German war production adapted itself skilfully to these requirements. On the one hand ways were found for evading the spirit while conforming to the letter of the Treaty; in particular the substitution of light metals for iron and steel and the use of the technique of welding instead of riveting armour plates rendered the weight restrictions imposed by the Treaty largely out of date.[1] On the other hand, various illegal armaments production units were disguised under innocent-sounding titles; as for example when the Rheinmetall Company opened an office for the construction of artillery and successfully represented it to the world as an office for constructing railway trucks.[2]

But the future army would need far more than simply a supply of weapons and ammunition. It must also have transport and all sorts of other equipment. This could be produced openly since it ostensibly served a peaceful purpose. All that was necessary was that it should be produced on a sufficient scale. The method adopted here was that of subsidies. During the second half of the twenties hundreds of millions of marks were paid out by the State to automobile manufacturers, shipbuilders, aero-engine makers, and the like, to enable them to produce on a scale far in excess of peace-time needs or profitable sales. Subsidies were also granted to steel and copper manufacturers, so that they might produce the requisite stocks of basic raw materials against the moment when rearmament could come out into the open, and to the makers of chemical fertilizers and textile growers so

[1] The outstanding example of this device was, of course, the construction of the 'pocket battleships', which were designed to fulfil the functions of heavy armoured cruisers while in weight remaining in the light cruiser class as demanded by the Treaty. The use of similar methods as applied to tanks was described by Dr. Walter Roland (who had been head of the Central Committee for Tanks) in a broadcast from Berlin on June 10, 1943.

[2] See the lecture of one of Rheinmetall's engineers, Dr. Karl Waninger, as reported in the *Völkischer Beobachter* of April 15, 1943.

that when the time came Germany might be more nearly self-sufficient in food and clothing than she had been in 1914.

A further point was to make sure that German rearmament and military training when it could afford to come out into the open should be from the technical point of view completely up to date. This presented no special difficulties in the case of weapons whose manufacture was permitted inside Germany. The firms concerned were merely told to use some of the subsidies they received for technical research and experiment. But in the use of the forbidden categories of weapons—notably military aeroplanes and submarines—the problem was more difficult. A German factory could hardly produce an experimental model of a new military aeroplane, nor a German shipyard launch an up-to-date submarine, without arousing comment; still less could future flying and naval instructors be trained in the use of these weapons under the eyes of the Inter-Allied Military Control Commission. It therefore became necessary for this part of the work to get help from outside. That help was forthcoming. The Junkers firm was allowed to set up a factory in Russia in the early twenties, the Dornier firm did the same in Switzerland, the Heinkel firm in Sweden; and it is known that at least one submarine was built by German technicians in Spain. One may presume that in the case of the three ex-neutral countries, or at any rate of Sweden and Switzerland, the work was done without the knowledge of the governments concerned. After all the German aircraft industry was ostensibly concerned only with the production of planes for civilian use, and while it might seem odd to locate factories for such purposes outside the territory of the Reich, yet nothing could be proved as to the real purpose behind it. It is not known how far any of these factories actually supplied Germany with finished war weapons. But they certainly gave her the chance of evolving prototypes, experimenting with new models, and training technical staff.

In the case of Russia, however, the matter went much farther. Not merely were planes built for Germany and by Germans on Russian soil; by a secret agreement between the military authorities of the two countries, concluded as early as 1921, the German militia was able to send flying personnel to a special aviation school a few miles outside Moscow; German soldiers were trained in the use of tanks and artillery of the latest model; full-dress German Army manœuvres were held for practising and testing the use of the weapons which the Treaty of Versailles had prohibited. In return the Germans gave Russia expert advice and help in rearing the infant Red Army. Thus while the propagandists were preaching anti-Bolshevism and the gangsters of the Free Corps and later of the National Socialist formations were murdering German Communists, the General Staffs of the two countries were helping to build up each other's strength. No doubt the German General Staff, in its blind underestimation of Russian military ability, thought it was getting the better of the bargain.

Finally, the planners of Germany's rearmament had learned that under modern conditions an army must have behind it an industrial machine prepared and organized to the last detail. That fact had not been fully grasped in the First World War. German industry had not been from the outset geared to the needs of the fighting services, and some experts held that the failure in this respect was responsible for Germany's having missed victory in the early months and years of the war. Long before the fighting was over books and articles had been published discussing the plans which must be made for the Second World War (on the assumption that the war then in progress would end at the best inconclusively), and in one of the most influential of these, written by Colonel Buch-Müller, special emphasis was laid on the need for fuller economic and industrial preparedness.[1] Now, in the conditions of the twenties, this matter became of quite exceptional importance. So long as Germany was attempting to hide her rearmament plans the work of the German war industry, though vital, could only be preliminary. Weapons could be produced, but not on nearly a sufficient scale for the needs of the future German Army. At some stage, therefore, the policy of concealment must be abandoned. But to rearm openly must be expected to have repercussions on Germany's enemies. At the very least they would surely start rearming themselves. And therefore it was essential that when the moment came for throwing off the mask, the German war industry should be able *at once* to produce at full capacity and

[1] This book was first published anonymously towards the end of 1916. Its title was *The Next War*. The author also stressed the need for more thorough *psychological* preparations than had been carried out before 1914— a lesson which Hitler and his associates took very much to heart; see below, pp. 97 ff. and Chapter VI.

with all possible speed. Then Germany could strike, and strike crushingly, while her opponents were still in the middle of their preparations. That was the plan—and it clearly required that German industry as a whole must be, so to speak, *potentially* mobilized during the period in which rearmament was not openly admitted.

So the war planners set to work. The Ministry of Defence appointed an 'economic staff' which in conjunction with the industrialists' organization, the 'Reich Association of German Industry', worked out detailed plans for the war output of every factory. The various firms received undated orders for definite quantities of the goods they were to supply. Each manager knew that when the industrial mobilization day came he would be expected to deliver that quantity of goods within a specified number of weeks or months; he also knew exactly from what source he would get the necessary raw materials, what the transport arrangements would be, and whether he would be required to expand his productive capacity.

So when the National Socialists took control they found ready for them not merely the nucleus of an army, trained in the use of the most modern weapons, but also an industrial machine which could be transformed at a moment's notice into a war machine. The heavy industrialists and their associates did far more for Hitler than merely help him into power; they also gave him the instruments whereby he could use that power for the warlike and aggressive ends for which they, and he, were working.[1]

4.

That Germany was already rearming in the twenties was of course known to the Allies, though they may not have realized, or would not believe, how thoroughly and systematically the work was being done. Why, then, did they not take steps to prevent it? Why, at the very least, did they not prepare themselves against the challenge which they would one day have to face? Partly for reasons discussed earlier in this chapter. They were at odds with one another: France was tired and disunited, Britain was wrestling with economic depression, America did not feel herself threatened. In addition, however, the Allies had

For a further illustration of how the National Socialists simply built on ground already prepared for them see below, pp. 90 f.

every reason to believe that the war aspirations of the men behind the scenes were not shared by the masses of the German
people. In 1926 a Member of the Reichstag, Philipp Scheide-
mann, had discovered the arrangements in force for building
aeroplanes and training crews in Russia. This revelation caused
an immense sensation in Germany, and the reaction of the
ordinary German was thoroughly hostile. Two years later,
when the question of building a new battle-cruiser came up
before the Reichstag, the proposal, though entirely in conformity with the Treaty of Versailles, was violently opposed by
the left-wing parties and was only in the end forced through
with the utmost difficulty. To the outside world it did not look
as though the militarists would get their way. Germany was in
theory a democratic State. At the head of its Government was
Stresemann, a man whom the Allies did not suspect of planning
a Second World War. As early as 1925 they had shown, in the
Locarno Pact, that they were willing and anxious to be friendly
with Germany and to forget the distinction between 'ex-Allied'
and 'ex-enemy' countries. They felt, in short, that the best hope
for the future peace of Europe lay in strengthening Stresemann's
hands with his own people; so instead of taking measures to stop
the process of rearmament behind the scenes they went to the
other extreme, evacuated the Rhineland almost five years before
the time laid down by the Treaty, and withdrew the Military
Control Commission. Alas, the only result was to make the work
of the war planners that much easier: the constitutional Government of Germany was not strong enough to enforce a policy of
peace upon the fanatics behind the scenes.[1]

Moreover there were two further factors which the Allies, and
perhaps also the German Government, had failed to take into
consideration.

One was the success of the propagandists inside Germany. I
have, in an earlier chapter, expressed my conviction that propaganda can only be efficacious if it appeals to feelings that already
exist among its intended victims. Judged by this test the ordinary German was an excellent subject for the propaganda of the
militarists. We have already seen how he was feeling: on the one

---

[1] The real position of Stresemann is a matter on which there will always
be room for discussion; for my part I see no reason for questioning his
sincerity as a man who desired Germany to achieve greatness by peaceful
means.

hand sincerely anxious for peace, on the other hand humiliated and resentful because of Germany's defeat. The propagandists made it their business to play on this latter emotion. They set out to persuade their fellow-countrymen that Germany had been treated shamefully and monstrously by the Allies and must some day reassert herself and restore her 'honour'. To this they added a steady stream of attacks against both Communism and demo-cracy—the former as being in some vague but horrible sense evil, the latter as being inefficient and weak. For different reasons both these lines of propaganda struck chords in the minds of their hearers. The abuse of democracy in particular was welcome to many simple Germans who were bewildered by the new and difficult world in which they found themselves, not by nature politically minded, reluctant to take on themselves the degree of individual responsibility which a true democracy de-mands from its citizens. The propagandists did their work well. By the end of the twenties there was widespread scepticism of the possibility of running the German State efficiently along the lines of the Weimar Republic. Younger people in particular were disposed to despise it as incompetent and out of date: for there had been no effective reform of the educational system (despite well-meaning efforts on the part of some ministers) and at school they had been in many cases taught by schoolmasters of the old type, out of textbooks which still taught the glories of Germany's world mission. These boys and girls formed the main support of the growing National Socialist movement. But the point of view they embodied was not confined either to the young people or to the National Socialist Party. It formed at least an *element* in the mental and emotional make-up of a majority of the whole people.

Even so it was not certain till the very end of the twenties that the propagandists would succeed in their task. So long as Germany was reasonably prosperous in the economic sense, there was a good prospect that the widespread desire for peace and international friendship would win the day and that the Allied policy of friendliness towards the German people and its constitutional rulers would be triumphantly justified.

But then came the economic crisis—as unexpected by the statesmen of Europe and America as it was devastating in its effects. The propagandists now had a magnificent new weapon with which to belabour the 'System'—the fact, namely, that it had failed to prevent the worst wave of unemployment in the history of the Reich. With that the battle for the soul of the German people was finally and irretrievably lost. Here again, when Hitler came to power he found that a large part of his work was already done for him: the majority, perhaps even the great majority, of his fellow-countrymen, though still wanting peace, were prepared to accept and support a policy which could only lead to war.

The other factor which the statesmen of Europe overlooked was the effect of the inflation period upon the social structure of Germany.

The inflation was the answer of German finance to the French occupation of the Ruhr. Up till the end of 1922 the mark, though depreciated, was no more so than the currencies of most European countries, and there would have been no insuperable difficulty in stabilizing it at a level corresponding with its current purchasing power. All that was necessary was to see that the budget balanced; whatever troubles might arise over reparations payments and their transference to the creditor countries, at least there would have been no runaway internal inflation.[1] Balancing the budget would indeed have entailed severe and even Draconian tax measures. But it could certainly have been done if the financial authorities had really wanted to do it.

That, however, is precisely the point. They did *not* really want to balance the budget. Apart from the specific measures taken to counter the occupation of the Ruhr—the suspension of deliveries in kind, the encouragement of passive resistance in the

---

[1] This is a proposition of vital importance. So long as the German Government saw to it that its revenues were sufficient to cover its expenditure (including sums due in reparations), so long there could be no large increase in the quantity of money and credit in circulation and the country's monetary situation would remain fundamentally stable. If the Allies attempted to *transfer* to themselves (as opposed to leaving on Allied account inside Germany) a larger proportion of reparations than could be covered by the value of net exports, then there would indeed be a threat to the *foreign exchanges* (as was recognized in the provisions of the Dawes Plan, which limited transfers in terms of what the exchanges could stand); the mark would become worth less *in terms of foreign currencies*. But that that need not have involved a fall in its *internal* value—its purchasing power over goods and services inside Germany—is shown by what happened in Great Britain in the autumn of 1931, when the pound went off the gold standard, became depreciated in terms of the dollar, the Reichsmark, and other foreign currencies, and yet prices in England remained completely stable and even fell.

occupied districts, the payment of subsistence allowances to thousands of striking workers; measures the wisdom or unwisdom of which is not our present concern—apart from all this, the people in charge of Germany's finances seem to have been positively anxious to throw the country's monetary system into chaos. They made no attempt to balance the budget; they printed banknotes with profusion and alacrity; they allowed public expenditure to rise greatly while making no effort to increase public revenues—and the mounting deficits were covered by printing more money. How far they fully realized what they were doing is doubtful. They may perhaps have *thought* that this was just a spectacular means of demonstrating to the Allies the impossibility of paying reparations. If so they must have been grievously disappointed by the upshot. For the Dawes Plan, introduced when the inflationary snowball was well under way, found it unnecessary to reduce the total Reparations Bill. And in fact Germany went on paying reparations during and after the inflation period at precisely the rates already determined.

The suggestion of the propagandists, therefore, that the inflation in Germany was due to the harsh reparations policy of the Allies—or alternatively to the machinations of a malignant group of Jewish international financiers—is completely without foundation. Allied policy on reparations was in many ways stupid and short-sighted, as I have tried to show in the first part of this chapter. But one thing for which it was *not* responsible was the German inflation. As for the other, the familiar, suggestion of the propagandists, it is sufficient to point out that the individuals immediately connected with carrying through the inflation were Helfferich the Finance Minister and Havenstein the President of the Reichsbank—both of them pure flowers of aggressive 'Aryan' German nationalism.

No, throughout this whole period the control of the German currency remained exclusively and entirely in the hands of the German Government, as was shown clearly in 1924 when with the appointment of Schacht the Government decided at last that a stable currency was after all a national asset. Within a few weeks, and without any assistance from outside, a new mark was established and the nightmare of inflation banished.

The policy of Germany's monetary authorities from the beginning of 1923 till the spring of 1924 was, in fact, at best an ignorant and irresponsible gesture of petty spite against France. At worst it was something much more sinister; it was an integral part of the great conspiracy against the German people.

For the inflation had the effect of ruining the whole class of small property owners who had been the backbone of the German middle class and a source of stability and strength to the nation as a whole. These people relied on their savings, their small investments, their insurance policies, their war-loan holdings. By the end of the inflation these had disappeared and they were left destitute or reduced to the level of a new, black-coated proletariat.

And who gained from the inflation? To some extent, indeed, peasants and small business men, who if they had mortgages on their properties or owed debts in money terms, found that the inflation had wiped these out. But chiefly the big industrialists, who no longer had to allocate a large share of their gross profits in paying interest to their bondholders. The inflation period was a golden era for these men; as it was, too, for the heavily indebted big landowners of eastern Germany. Not merely were they able to raise still further their own already high standard of life, they were also in a position to spend immense sums on *political* ends—the financing of secret rearmament, payments to private free corps of their own, money for spreading unrest and nationalist propaganda, subsidies to the National Socialists.

In short, the inflation resulted in a shift of the whole balance of power in Germany—away from the classes that might be expected to want peace and a quiet life and in favour of those who, on grounds of political conviction as well as of economic interest, throve on rearmament and looked forward to a Second World War.

Thus everything conspired to nullify the hopes of the Treaty-makers. On the Allied side disunity, failure to understand the economic implications of the settlement, and reluctance to take action in time against the menace of German rearmament; on the German side resentment at the fact of defeat, malignant propaganda, and the shift of power into the hands of the war-planners; and to crown all this the onset of the greatest economic depression the world had ever known: these were the factors which undermined the peace and gave the National Socialists their chance. America went her own way; Britain vacillated

between her rights and responsibilities as a European Power
and her ties with her own Empire and the Dominions overseas;
France built her Maginot Line and despairingly sat behind it,
waiting apathetically for a denouement which she alone among
the Allies had the vision to foresee; and the men behind the
scenes in Germany went on thoroughly and systematically, by
research, organization, and propaganda, preparing the way for
the Second World War.

V

SIX AND A HALF YEARS OF NATIONAL SOCIALISM

1.

HITLER came to power as the result of a bargain between him and the old-fashioned nationalists. We need not go into the details of the story. At the time National Socialism seemed to be on the decline; its leaders were in despair; popular opinion seemed to be swinging to the parties of the left. The German nationalists became alarmed. Heavy industrialists feared the threat to their own wealth and power. The landowners of the north-east were faced with the prospect that their corruption in connexion with the Government funds for the relief of their indebtedness would come to light. Though these people disliked the National Socialists, they saw in Hitler their last chance. So finances were supplied from the coffers of heavy industry and the landowners used their influence with Hindenburg to have Hitler appointed Chancellor. Reluctantly Hindenburg consented.

Hitler's first step was to obtain a majority in the Reichstag. This he did by the simple method of arresting the representatives of the parties who might oppose him. He then suspended the Constitution and settled down in earnest to the work which lay ahead: preparing Germany for war.

There were four main tasks to be accomplished.

The first was to build up Germany's internal military strength. That Hitler attached the utmost importance to this from the moment of his seizure of power was subsequently fully and proudly admitted. In his speech of September 1, 1939, he announced that since 1933 he had spent over 90 milliard marks on armaments alone; and two and a half years later he added a list of the stages through which National Socialist Germany had passed on the road to complete preparedness. The first three stages were described in the following words: 'In 1934 Germany began to produce armaments on an all-out basis; in 1935 I introduced general conscription; in 1936 I ordered the re-occupation of the Rhineland.' We need not trace the course of these events in detail: they are familiar and undisputed.

But one consequence of rearmament—an incidental but highly welcome one—was that it soon led to the disappearance of unemployment in Germany. Again we do not need to go into details. Suffice it that by 1936 or 1937 labour in Germany, so far from being excessively abundant, had become scarce—so scarce that women were now required in the factories and the earlier National Socialist slogan that their place was in the home had to be quietly but firmly forgotten.

By curing unemployment the National Socialists won the deep gratitude of millions of labourers and their families; in fact the increase in German industrial activity was the main, almost the only reason for the loyal support the German working classes gave to Hitler during the terrible years that were to come. Even late on in the war German prisoners, including many who in other respects were critical of, possibly actively hostile to, Hitler's conduct and policy, would often say to their interrogators: 'After all, he did give us jobs when we were down and out.'

It is therefore important to underline that the curing of unemployment in Germany between 1933 and 1937 was not due to the rearmament programme as *rearmament*, but as a *programme*. Any large-scale expenditure on public works would have had the same effect. The vital thing was that private enterprise had failed to provide the necessary work and the State stepped in and took its place. Had Hitler spent his 90 milliard marks, or even a fraction of that sum, on work designed to improve the amenities of life in German towns and on German farms, had he carried through the large rebuilding schemes on which he was so genuinely keen, not merely would unemployment have been cured but in addition the standard of life of the German people would have been permanently raised.

Moreover, the financial technique employed by the National Socialists in their rearmament programme—the technique of 'forward finance' by way of works-creation and other bills—was itself simply an adaptation and extension of a method already introduced in the form of tax-exemption certificates under Papen's short-lived Government in 1932. Papen was gone before the results of his policy began to show themselves, and the National Socialists were able to reap where Papen's financial advisers had sown. But there is no question that unemployment in Germany would have fallen in 1933 and subsequent years even had there been no Hitler and no immense rearmament

programme. It should not be forgotten that by the time the
National Socialists came to power the depression was lifting the
whole world over. Different countries adopted different
methods of helping on the good work. In Britain the improvement depended primarily on a boom in house and road building, for which private and local public enterprise were jointly
responsible.[1] In the United States the emphasis was rather on
'public works' in the stricter sense—that is to say, on govern-
ment-financed programmes of land improvement, hydro-
electric schemes, and the like. In neither country was the
elimination of unemployment as rapid or as complete as it was
in Germany. But their example is sufficient to show that it
would have been perfectly possible for Hitler, had his primary
object been to overcome the economic depression, to achieve
that object by less wasteful and warlike methods than he in fact
adopted.

That is not to say that rearmament was completely unjustifi-
able. In Britain, at any rate, there was at the time no disposition
to quarrel with Germany's right to the means of her own self-
defence, even at the expense of breaking the provisions of the
Treaty of Versailles. We shall discuss this point at a later stage.
At the moment what matters is to underline that the objective of
the Nazis in their rearmament programme was *not* the cure of
unemployment as such but the creation of a strong army fully
equipped for aggressive action.

2.

Hitler's second task was to make Germany less vulnerable than
she had been in 1914 to the effects of blockade. We saw in the
last chapter how even in the twenties German endeavours were
directed to the goal of self-sufficiency in the production of foodstuffs. The National Socialists continued and extended this
policy. The Four Years Plan was specifically and openly
designed to make Germany independent of the outer world in
respect of a series of vital war materials. In announcing the
Four Years Plan at the Nuremberg Party Rally in 1936 Hitler

[1] Britain's record in eliminating unemployment during these years was
poorer than Germany's. The published figures exaggerated the difference,
indeed, since the British returns included all those temporarily unemployed,
if only for a couple of days, whereas the German returns did not. But even
allowing for that, it is clear that the British Government did less than it could
have done to overcome the depression by a programme of public works.

defined its purpose as follows: 'Within four years Germany must be wholly independent of the outside world in all materials which can by any means be produced at home through German ability and the efforts of our chemical, engineering and mining industries.' Low-grade iron-ore deposits were developed at home so that Germany should not have to lean upon the iron production of Lorraine or Sweden; plants were set up for extracting motor fuel from coal; a crushing tariff was placed upon natural rubber so as to encourage the production of buna; home-produced staple fibre and rayon was substituted for imported cotton, wool and silk. The new product was in every case far more expensive, and in some cases appreciably inferior in quality, than the old product it ousted. Thus it cost at least three times as much to produce a gallon of synthetic petrol from coal as to purchase a gallon of natural petrol from Rumania or Venezuela, and not less than six times as much to produce a pound of buna as to purchase a pound of raw rubber from Malaya. The whole plan was in fact wholly 'uneconomic'. It directly (and in the case of clothing visibly) lowered the standard of life of the German people. The case in favour of it was, of course, that it helped to equip Germany for standing up to a second world war.

This was not often admitted in so many words, though one cannot say that any particularly violent attempts were made to conceal it. As a rule autarky was taken for granted by the propagandists as a good thing in itself—which, indeed, was tantamount to an admission of its real purpose, since it is not obvious why autarky should have been desirable, in view of its deleterious effects on the national standard of living, except from the point of view of war and war preparations. Sometimes, however, one or other of two arguments were put forward in its defence. The first argument was that the more self-sufficient Germany could become the less exposed she would be to world trade influences and the less susceptible, therefore, to future economic depressions. We do not need to spend much time on this particular contention. In itself it is not without force, when one bears in mind the chaotic conditions of international economic life at the time and the unwillingness of the Great Powers to seek an international remedy for what is after all an international evil. But it would not be advanced as a reason for retiring from world trade altogether, except by people who were in favour of doing that anyway on other grounds. The economic losses involved in autarky are clearly far greater than the economic gains, especially when one bears in mind that it is always possible for a country faced with the threat of depression to take the necessary steps to provide employment by a programme of peaceful public works.

The other defence of autarky was that it had been *forced* on Germany, contrary to her own wishes: had become a necessity owing to her lack of access to foreign markets and the refusal of the Western Powers to trade fairly with her. This argument calls for more extended treatment.

It is true that the trend of events in the thirties was unfavourable to Germany's full participation in world trade. The reason for that was partly the further growth of economic nationalism in the western world and in particular the conversion of Great Britain and the British Self-governing Dominions to a policy of Imperial Preferences which put obstacles in the way of trade between the British Empire and all non-British countries. That policy was in my view foolish and short-sighted. It aroused much irritation in the United States, Italy, and elsewhere (as well as Germany), and while its apologists could point out that the tariff wall round Great Britain and her Crown Colonies was still substantially lower than those erected by any of the other Great Powers, yet there *was* a wall and to that extent there came to be substance in the complaint that Germany was being directly injured by having no colonies of her own.[1]

But far more important as a factor hampering Germany's foreign trade was the wall she had erected around *herself*—the wall of foreign trade control and exchange restrictions. We have seen how these originated: they were the immediate result of the financial crisis of 1931. Faced in July with a flight of foreign capital which would soon have denuded the Reichsbank of its reserves, the German authorities had to choose between two alternatives: either to abandon the gold standard (the alternative selected by Britain two months later); or else to maintain the gold parity of the mark and instead to set up machinery for determining in detail which payments to foreign creditors

[1] The colonial question is dealt with in some detail later on (see pp. 111 ff., 156 ff., below, and cf. pp. 55 ff. above). Here it is enough to note that while the possession of colonies would have increased Germany's ability to be self-sufficient in peace-time, it would have made no direct contribution towards autarky in war, when she had to reckon on being denied the use of the seas.

should be authorized and which refused. Now to have gone off the gold standard would have been a serious shock to German public opinion, which would doubtless have taken for granted that a second inflation period was imminent. Therefore the German authorities, with the consent of Germany's creditors, adopted the method of foreign exchange control. The purpose of this, as we have seen, was *simply* to tide over the immediate crisis: to see to it that no more foreign capital should be withdrawn from Germany than could be met by current foreign exchange holdings. And it was certainly the hope and expectation of Germany's foreign creditors that as international confidence returned the restrictions would gradually be relaxed and finally removed altogether. Whether this could have been achieved, as things turned out, without the devaluation of the mark in terms of gold, is highly doubtful. But once the immediate crisis was over a devaluation of this sort need not have held any terrors for Germany. Not merely had the British experience shown that a currency could be detached from gold without losing any of its internal stability, but the devaluation of sterling had carried with it a corresponding and almost simultaneous devaluation of a number of other countries, which formed the so-called 'Sterling group'. As time passed an ever larger group of countries followed Britain's example, and improved their internal economic situation as well as their foreign trade prospects by so doing; while another group of countries, headed by the United States, while not formally breaking loose from gold, achieved the same result by reducing the 'gold content' of their currency. Under these circumstances it was both pedantic and self-hurting for Germany to refuse to follow suit. Her attitude was that of a member of a column of marching soldiers who, when all his comrades have changed step, refuses to follow suit: in the monetary field Germany was almost literally 'out of step' with the rest of the world; a fact which was a source of minor inconvenience to the other countries and of major inconvenience and damage to herself.[1]

But the National Socialists soon decided that they did not *want* to bring to an end the system of foreign exchange restrictions.

[1] German readers can find a development of this argument, couched in discreet language, in an article of mine which appeared in the *Deutscher Volkswirt* in September 1935 under the title 'Was heisst Waehrungsstabilisierung?'

On the contrary they welcomed and drastically extended it. From their point of view it had three important advantages.

First it enabled Germany to continue defaulting on her foreign obligations. We need not go into the details: it is enough to say that from 1933 onwards Germany's foreign creditors only received sums due to them if, and to the extent that, it was to Germany's immediate advantage that they should be paid.[1]

Secondly, it put Germany in a position to bargain with each foreign country separately on the terms and structure of trade relations with that country; which meant that in all cases where Germany was economically stronger than the bargaining partner she could force the latter to adapt its economic life to her needs —could convert it, in fact, into the willing or unwilling servant of her war production. Moreover the economic control Germany obtained in this way over her weaker neighbours carried with it far-reaching political implications. The countries concerned—for example in south-eastern Europe—could not afford to quarrel with a country to whom they were committed as the one market for their agricultural exports; and therefore they inevitably pursued a more or less open pro-National-Socialist policy. From their point of view, therefore, what had looked like a tolerable commercial bargain was the gateway to something approaching political slavery.

And thirdly, the control of foreign exchange represented an admirable line of approach to the vital task of controlling German industry itself. The Government alone decided for what imports the necessary means of payment would be made available; and therefore the Government had the last word as to what goods were to be imported at all—in other words, by the mere granting, or refusing, of foreign exchange the National Socialists could compel any firm which depended on overseas sources for its raw material to direct its production along the lines they desired. Similarly, industries dependent on export

[1] From this point of view Great Britain was fortunate. She had always bought more from Germany than she had sold to Germany, and she was therefore in a position to refuse the excess imports unless a proportion of their purchasing price was used for the repayment of her frozen debts. The fact that she used this bargaining weapon, even instituting a 'compulsory clearing' system for the enforcement of her terms, roused immense indignation among the National Socialists. But they were for once powerless: they badly needed sterling balances for other purposes and thus could not afford to fall back on the only alternative open to them, namely reducing German exports to Britain to the level of British exports to Germany.

markets for their sales could be directed to particular lines of production or to particular countries for the disposal of their products—again in terms of what the National Socialists considered to be in the interest of their own policy.

Judged by subsequent standards this type of control may seem mild and circuitous. But the National Socialists were not at the outset ready to apply to every German producer the ruthless methods of direct compulsion which later became second nature to them. They had to develop their apparatus of control gradually. And the restrictions on foreign exchange dealings which they found already in existence when they came into power offered them an excellent starting-point.

Thus the wall of exchange restrictions which came to hem Germany in during the National Socialist era was a wall which they for their own purposes strengthened and heightened. To offer it as an excuse for pursuing a policy of autarky was merely a propaganda device—an inversion of the true relationship. Autarky was the end in view; foreign trade restrictions were only means to that end.

3.

The third main task facing the National Socialists when they came into power was to groom and discipline the German people for the ordeal that lay before them. They had to be made to support the National Socialist policy wherever it led: to economic and industrial mobilization there had to be added political and psychological mobilization.

The weapons at the disposal of the National Socialists for this purpose were four: terror, bribes, habituation to war-time conditions, and propaganda. The facts about the first three of these weapons are within the recollection of all Germans and are self-explanatory. On the one hand opponents of the régime were murdered or thrown into concentration camps, while potential opponents were silenced by the fear of the Gestapo. In this way the National Socialists sought to ensure that no opposition should have a chance of organizing itself or even of becoming vocal. That they did not kill opposition altogether is by now well known, nor can they have hoped for that; but they succeeded in making it powerless to interfere with their plans.

On the other hand, the ordinary non-political minded German working man was encouraged in his support of the régime by small concessions and amenities such as 'Strength through Joy' holidays. These were for the most part more than sufficient to keep him contented, especially in view of his feeling of gratitude to the régime for having cured unemployment. Nor do I suggest that the attention paid to the interests of the working classes by such organizations as the German Labour Front was wholly insincere: there is, on the contrary, every reason to believe that some of the older members of the Party—in particular Robert Ley, for all his grotesqueness—had a genuine desire to see the German working man happy and contented.

At the other extreme big business was mollified and stimulated by huge armaments contracts and by the knowledge that the National Socialists were carrying out the policy for which it had been working ever since 1919. The peasant was encouraged to support the régime by efforts to raise the prices of his products and to cut middlemen's profits—and here too the sincerity of some of the National Socialist leaders is hardly open to question. The civil servant was offered an unrivalled opportunity of showing his power of organizing his fellow citizens. The small or medium-sized manufacturer, though losing most of his freedom, might hope for a profitable government contract. In fact the only classes which were offered nothing in the way of bribes were the professional classes—lawyers, doctors, university professors, pastors—in whose work and standards the National Socialists were not in the least interested; and the great mass of the lower middle class—clerks, shopkeepers, one-man-firms, and the like—about whose loyalty the National Socialists did not need to worry since it was precisely from this class that they had drawn their chief support before they acceded to power.

Thirdly, the masses of the German people were taught to think and act as though they were already at war. To the young men and women that meant conscription and labour service with military discipline. To the children it meant on the one hand the para-military activities of the Hitler Youth and the League of German Girls, and on the other hand indoctrination in school classes with the idea that war was the natural state of affairs so long as any of Germany's rivals still survived. To the population as a whole it meant air-raid exercises, inferior food and clothing, increased hours of work, heavier taxes, compulsory listening to Hitler's speeches, the renunciation of the right to live one's life as one wished. It is no exaggeration to say that by the time of the Munich crisis the ordinary German had already learnt to think of himself as being a member of an armed fortress, accepting privations and restrictions on his liberty as self-evident, ready for still further privations and restrictions as soon as his leaders gave the word of command.

Moreover, the restrictions and privations were not confined to the material sphere. They applied equally to the things of the mind. The evil effects of National Socialism on Germany's educational system are too well known to require analysis here. Doubtless the leading National Socialists, who were for the most part relatively unlearned men, were unaware of the importance of education for achieving national greatness; perhaps, too, they were inspired by a feeling of envy at the high status accorded by earlier generations in Germany to universities and places of higher learning and research. But beyond that they saw in the objective pursuit of truth a direct threat to their own hold over the German people. Anybody who could and would think for himself was likely to be a lukewarm supporter—might become an active opponent.[1] Therefore intellectualism had to be branded as a source of weakness, unworthy of National Socialist manhood. Therefore, too, the German people had to be as far as possible cut off from intellectual contacts with the outside world—by prohibitions on the import of unwelcome books and periodicals and, at a later stage, by imposing penalties on listening to foreign radio stations. In these ways the German people was to be as far as possible *intellectually* autarkic; it was to depend for its views and convictions solely upon what the National Socialists chose to provide for it.

Which brings us to the fourth weapon used for the psychological mobilization of Germany—the weapon of propaganda. It was essential for the National Socialists, if they were to have the whole-hearted and unfaltering support of the masses of the

---

[1] I remember talking a few years before the war to the headmaster of a secondary school in a small German town—an elderly man of liberal political leanings who believed in encouraging his pupils to think for themselves. He used to conduct discussions in his classes on the reasons for the various actions of the National Socialists. He found that while the less intellectual boys found such discussions merely boring, their standpoint being that it was unnecessary for them to understand the grounds for the Fuehrer's actions, any pupil who had an aptitude for reasoning and argument not merely greatly enjoyed these classes but invariably became in one direction or another critical of National Socialist policy.

German people during the coming war, that the latter should be completely satisfied of its justice and of their right to wage a war in a just cause. If any suspicion were felt that the war was a war of aggression and conquest, the fighting spirit of the German people would be seriously, perhaps disastrously affected. Therefore until all such suspicions had been eliminated (except of course among the incorrigible minority which must in any case be gagged or destroyed) Germany could not be said to be fully mobilized for action.

So the propagandists set to work with a will. To a large extent they concentrated on themes on which a lot of work had been done already by nationalist elements during the twenties. The object of the stab-in-the-back legend, of the continuing-blockade legend, of the Fourteen-Points legend, of the reparations, inflation, and world-slump legends was to convince the ordinary German that he had been monstrously ill-used by envious and unscrupulous foreigners and that it was his right and duty to avenge himself. The object of the glorification of war as a propaganda theme was to reconcile him to the idea that the best if not the only way of avenging himself was by the sword. The object of depicting the Germans as a master people and of demanding the preservation of its racial purity was to give him a sense of pride and strength and unity with fellow Germans. The object of the anti-Jewish, anti-Communist, and anti-plutocrat propaganda was to give him an apparently concrete victim for his righteous wrath—and at the same time (in the case of the anti-Semitism drive) to provide the National Socialists with a convenient scapegoat on to which they could pin the blame for any of their own failures and so direct public indignation away from themselves. Finally the National Socialist propagandists utilized a further set of themes designed to show that Germany was even now threatened; that there were foes outside her frontiers who, not content with past wrongs, were preparing to renew the attack, and that unless Germany fought and destroyed these foes the very basis of her existence as a nation would be denied to her. The object of this line was, of course, to convince the ordinary German that when war did come it would be purely a war of self-defence and self-preservation; and therefore a war in a just cause. To which was added the rider that the foes in question were weak and degenerate, so that the issue of the war could not be in doubt.

We shall come back to the content of this last group of themes in the next chapter. The point here is the function that they, along with all the rest of the National Socialist propaganda lines listed above, were intended to fulfil—the function, namely, of bringing about the psychological mobilization of the German people. For the National Socialists, in fact, Propaganda (as Hitler had said in *Mein Kampf*) was primarily and essentially a 'means to an end'.

Not that it was always so regarded in practice. On the contrary, many of the propagandists, from Hitler himself downward, genuinely believed in at least a substantial proportion of the theses on which they so passionately and repetitively expatiated. Later on, indeed, this became a source of disaster to Germany's war prospects, since on more than one crucial occasion Hitler based a far-reaching strategical decision on convictions—or 'intuitions'—inspired by his own propaganda rather than on an objective appraisal of the facts. But at the time the power of self-deception and self-infection was a source of additional strength to the propagandists. Just as they appealed to emotions that were already present, if often dormant, in the minds of their hearers, so they projected on to those hearers what they themselves had come firmly to believe. They were all the more persuasive through being at times sincere.

And so the German people was prepared, as German armaments and the German economic system were prepared, for the renewal of the struggle against the enemies of 1914.

4.

The fourth and last task during these six and a half years was to strengthen Germany externally—by building up a system of alliances with other totalitarian States, and by weakening the strategic position and strength of Germany's future enemies. The former task was accomplished by the formation of the Axis and the Anti-Comintern Pact, which between them gave Germany the support of two Great Powers and half a dozen smaller ones. The latter was accomplished by a series of coups coupled with pacts of non-aggression, guarantees of peaceful intentions, assurances of good faith, offers of enduring peace.

The objective of these coups was threefold: first to add to the territory of the Reich such areas as could be claimed to have a predominantly Germanic population, along with any non-Germanic territory which could be absorbed without prematurely bringing about a world war; secondly, to create confusion and disunion among the countries not immediately threatened; and thirdly, to confirm the loyalty of the German people to the régime by the achievement of brilliant and bloodless successes.

The salient facts must here be set out at some length, for they have a vital bearing on the question of the responsibility for the Second World War.

The first coup was the remilitarization of the Rhineland in March 1936. We are not at the moment concerned with the justice or injustice of this coup on its merits. The immediate point is that it was in direct contradiction of the Locarno agreements, in which Germany had undertaken not to break the Articles of the Treaty of Versailles concerning the status of the Rhineland.

But was the Third Reich bound by an agreement entered into during the Weimar period? Hitler himself had announced that he felt himself so bound. In his Reichstag speech ten months before, on May 21, 1935, he had said: 'The present German Government will scrupulously observe any voluntarily signed treaty even if concluded before its entry into office and power.' It was not disputed that the Locarno agreements had been signed 'voluntarily' by Germany; on the contrary, in the same speech Hitler said that the German Government would 'uphold and fulfil all obligations arising out of the Locarno treaty, so long as the other partners on their side are ready to stand by that pact'. And, he added, 'In respecting the demilitarized zone the German Government considers its action as a contribution to the pacification of Europe'.

As his excuse for nevertheless breaking the Locarno agreements Hitler pointed to the military pact between France and Russia. But, first, that had already been announced *before* the speech from which the above quotations are taken was delivered, and was indeed referred to in the same speech. In other words, Hitler formally reiterated his acceptance of the demilitarization of the Rhineland *in spite of* the doubts he later professed to feel about the compatibility of the Franco-Russian Pact with Locarno. And secondly, these doubts were not shared by any of the other Locarno signatories and when

Germany raised them France offered to submit the question to the International Court at The Hague—a suggestion which Germany turned down.

The reoccupation of the Rhineland was thus a direct contravention of undertakings entered into by the German Government and explicitly confirmed by Hitler himself. It was also a stepping-stone for further plans; for it meant that when Germany attacked France's allies in eastern and south-eastern Europe the French would no longer be able to come quickly and effectively to their aid.

No sooner were German soldiers in the Rhineland than Hitler stated categorically, 'We have no further territorial demands in Europe'.

The second coup was the annexation of Austria.

On January 30, 1934, Hitler had said in the Reichstag: 'The assertion that the German Reich intends to isolate the Austrian State is absurd. . . . I must categorically deny the further assertion . . . that an attack will be made on the Austrian State or is even being planned by the Reich.'

Nevertheless, on July 22, 1934, six months later, a National Socialist force operating from Munich carried out such an attack. They seized the Austrian Chancellery and murdered the Chancellor. The German Minister in Vienna was directly implicated. The attempt failed, however, and Austria retained her independence.

On May 21, 1935, Hitler said in the Reichstag: 'Germany has neither the intention nor the will to intervene in internal Austrian affairs, or to annex Austria and so join Austria to herself.'

On July 11, 1936, Hitler concluded an agreement with Austria which started by referring back to his speech of the year before and went on: 'The Government of the German Reich recognizes the full sovereignty of the Austrian Federal State. Each of the two Governments considers the internal political structure of the other country, *including the question of Austrian National Socialism*, as part of the internal affairs of that country, over which they will exercise no influence, *whether directly or indirectly*.'

Note especially the phrases which I have italicized. In February and March 1938 Hitler's demand for the *Anschluss* was based on the contention that the Austrians who wanted the *Anschluss*—namely the National Socialists—were in a majority but were being held down and oppressed by a tyrannous and oppressive government. At the same time he had instructed the National Socialists in Austria to make themselves as prominent as possible, and in particular to defy the Government's ban on public demonstrations and on the singing of the *Horst Wessel* song. But when the Austrian Chancellor offered to put the question of the *Anschluss* to a plebiscite Hitler at once changed his ground, demanded the postponement of the plebiscite, and gave the German Army the order to occupy the country. In an interview with an English journalist he actually cited the offer of a plebiscite as the *ground* for the invasion.

Thus apart from the invasion itself, Hitler broke the agreement of 1936 in three different ways. He fomented trouble inside the Austrian State. He used that trouble as an excuse for official interference in Austria's affairs. And he treated the proposal for a plebiscite—an Austrian internal affair, but one which would have shown up the hollowness of his own assertions—as an act of aggression and defiance, and ordered Schuschnigg to cancel it.

The annexation of Austria gave Germany complete control of communications with south-eastern Europe, encircled Czechoslovakia, and added nearly seven million people and considerable industrial and financial resources to Germany's war potential.

The third coup was the annexation of the Sudetenland.

On March 7, 1936, Hitler had said of the States of eastern and south-eastern Europe, specifically including Czechoslovakia, 'Germany has no wish to attack these States'.

On March 14, 1938, Goering, on behalf of Hitler, declared that Germany had no designs against the integrity of Czechoslovakia.[1]

During the subsequent months the Sudetenland National Socialist Party conducted a continuous agitation, inspired and directed (this was subsequently admitted) from Berlin.[2]

For a time the crisis seemed to die away, when France

---

[1] Reported in the official *Prager Presse*. Cf. Henderson, *Failure of a Mission*, p. 128!

[2] See, for example, the statement by Henlein quoted in the *Neues Wiener Tagblatt* for March 5, 1941.

declared her determination to come to Czechoslovakia's aid in the event of German aggression. The British Prime Minister, without giving a formal guarantee to Czechoslovakia, declared his view that a German attack was not likely to remain a purely local matter. But the tension soon flared up again, and at Munich Great Britain and France, having tried to save the integrity of the Czechoslovak State by peaceful means, climbed down and let Hitler have his way.

The annexation of the Sudetenland added a further three millions and more to the population of the Reich, along with highly developed industries, including the largest armaments factory in Europe. It also deprived the Czechs of their only defensible frontier to the north and west.

On September 26, three days before the Munich decision, Hitler declared in a speech at the Sport Palace in Berlin: 'I assured Mr. Chamberlain and I repeat the assurance now, that when this problem is solved there are no further territorial problems for Germany in Europe. . . . I further assured him that I shall then be no longer interested in the Czech State. And I guarantee him that. We do not want any Czechs.' On December 6 a declaration to the same effect was signed by Germany and France.

This assurance and guarantee was a fitting prelude to Hitler's fourth coup—the occupation of Bohemia and Moravia on March 15, 1939.

The fifth coup was the annexation of Memelland on March 22. It gave Germany complete economic control over Lithuania, and along with the occupation of Moravia and the de facto annexation of Danzig completed the encirclement of Poland.

The sixth coup was to have been the formal taking over of Danzig and the annexation of whatever parts of Poland Hitler had decided that he wanted.

In October 1933 Hitler had told the Polish Minister in Berlin: 'No one in Germany thinks of going to war with Poland over the Corridor.' In November 1933 he declared: 'Poland is a reality which nothing can change nor make to disappear.'

On January 26, 1934, Germany and Poland had entered into an agreement for the peaceful settlement of all disputes between them. The declaration embodying it contained the words: 'In no circumstances will they proceed to the application of force for the purpose of reaching a decision in such disputes.'

The two Governments bound themselves to observe this non-aggression pact for ten years.

In his Reichstag speech on May 21, 1935, Hitler said: 'We feel it unpleasant . . . that access to the sea accorded to a nation of 33 millions should cut through former territory of the Reich; but we recognize that it is unreasonable, because impossible, to dispute the question of access to the sea for so great a state.'

On January 30, 1939, Hitler described the non-aggression pact of 1934 as having been an invaluable contribution to peace, and added: 'During the troubled months of the past year the friendship between Germany and Poland has been one of the reassuring factors in the political life of Europe.'

On April 28 Germany denounced the non-aggression pact with Poland. The excuse offered was that Great Britain had in the meantime offered a guarantee of Poland's integrity. To this we shall come back in a moment: it is, however, obvious that it in no way affected the non-aggression pact.

On September 1 the German Army crossed the Polish frontier and German planes dropped bombs on Polish towns and villages. The question was no longer one of setting the stage for action. The curtain was up.[1]

Meanwhile on August 23 Germany had entered into a non-aggression pact with Russia. . . .

She had also concluded a non-aggression pact with Denmark on May 31, 1939, and had given assurances of friendship to Norway (April 6), Belgium (August 26), Holland (August 27), and Jugoslavia (March 1938). By her aid, too, a friendly Government had been established, after bitter civil war, in Spain.[2]

This is not, of course, a complete list of Hitler's broken pledges. For instance, on May 21, 1935, when full-scale rearmament had been under way for about a year, he declared 'The German Government has announced the extent of the creation of the new German defensive forces. It will under no circumstances depart therefrom.' Again, a month later, on June 18, 1935, Germany signed an agreement with Great

[1] Germany's handling of the Danzig crisis in August, 1939, is described at the beginning of Chapter VI.
[2] See further on Spain, below, pp. 121 f.

Britain which fixed 'permanently and definitely' the ratio of the tonnage of various classes of warship to be included in the two countries' navies. On April 28, 1939, Hitler denounced this agreement without notice. And the list could be prolonged.

For Hitler, in fact, a treaty was simply—and literally—a *ruse de guerre*. He himself on more than one occasion admitted this. On one occasion he bluntly declared 'We interpret treaties as we think fit and we do not submit to the judgement of others.' In an apostrophe to Mr. Chamberlain, who had pointed out that the invasion of Czechoslovakia in March 1939 was a breach of a freely and solemnly given pledge, he said with bitter sarcasm: 'I thank you, Herr Chamberlain, that you do not believe that I would ever be a traitor to my own people.'[1] In other words, no treaty was binding which might conflict with Germany's immediate national interests. As the British Ambassador to Berlin, Sir Nevile Henderson, expressed in his *Autobiography*, Hitler 'was ready to sign anything'. He would guarantee any frontier and conclude a non-aggression pact with anyone; nothing of this sort would restrict his freedom of action when the time came.[2]

In citing all this I am not at the moment concerned to criticize or condemn. Whatever we may think of the ethics of this procedure—whether or not we admit that ethical considerations have any place at all in international relations—at least the facts are clear and unmistakable. Right through these six and a half years Hitler used treaties and pledges and guarantees and assurances of friendship as a means of gaining his immediate ends. They proved an extremely effective

[1] February 24, 1940, on the occasion of the twentieth anniversary of the founding of the Party.

[2] Here is a story which illustrates perfectly the National Socialist attitude to treaties. A British diplomat in Berlin was having a talk with a high Nazi official. The subject came round to the Concordat with the Vatican about the rights of the Catholic Church in Germany. The Englishman was able to point out that every single item of that Concordat had been openly and flagrantly broken by the National Socialists. The Party official became impatient. 'Why are you, an Englishman, so interested in our relations with the Vatican? What has it to do with you?' 'We have a naval agreement with you', was the answer; 'it is natural that we should take an interest in your attitude to your own undertakings.' 'That's quite different', said the Official angrily, 'the Fuehrer has at the moment no intention whatever of breaking the naval agreement with England.'

In other words, do not have the impertinence to question the validity of a German promise until Germany herself decides that the time has come to break it!

instrument, for the time being. With their help he was able to divide his opponents and deal with them one by one: so that by the summer of 1939 Germany had obtained a stranglehold on the whole of central Europe, from the Baltic Sea to the Black Sea, and from the Rhine to the Vistula. Hitler's fourth main task was accomplished—the extension of Germany's power and resources outside the former frontiers of the Reich, in readiness for the coming war.

5.

But the technique had other consequences that were in the end to prove fatal to Hitler's hopes.

To understand these we must go back over the period from the National Socialist seizure of power and look at it from the point of view of the Western Powers. I may be forgiven if here I concentrate most of my attention on Great Britain, about whose attitude to the progress of National Socialism I can speak from personal experience.

We saw in the last chapter how feelings in Great Britain towards Germany had steadily improved during the twenties. There were a number of reasons for this: the fact that the war had caused England relatively little direct suffering, and had left behind it a correspondingly small legacy of bitterness and hatred; the desire to forget the past and to build for the future on the basis of enduring friendship; the impression brought back by soldiers of the Army of Occupation that the Germans and the British thought alike and got on well together; the belief that Germany under her new democratically organized Government was as anxious as Britain to make the peace an enduring one; the feeling of irritation with France for not sharing this faith; and above all the conviction that the Treaty of Versailles must be judged not by its success in exploiting Germany's defeat but by the extent to which it genuinely contributed to a lasting and just settlement. The average Englishman was, of course, largely ignorant of the contents of the Treaty or of the principles underlying it—not less ignorant than the average German was of the contents of the Fourteen Points and the extent to which they had been carried out. But on one or two points he had a vague feeling that the Treaty was unconstructive and even vengeful. The phrase referring to war guilt seemed unnecessarily provocative. Not that it ever occurred to him to doubt that Germany—or at any rate the German Government—was in fact guilty; but he did not see any point in making her sign a written statement to that effect. The Keynes controversy on the size of the Reparations Bill made him feel, though understanding nothing of the issues really involved, that perhaps the Allies had been rather grasping in their financial demands—an impression which the history of the reparations problem during the twenties seemed fully to confirm. Colonies? The average Englishman hardly felt that there was any 'injustice' in Germany's treatment on this issue, but neither, on the other hand, did he exclude the possibility of Germany's once again becoming a Colonial Power if she felt the matter to be important. Finally, though he approved of the disarmament of Germany, he assumed that that was simply a prelude to general disarmament.

The German propagandists, of course, made every effort to encourage this general attitude, both for its own sake and as a means of creating dissension between Great Britain and France. From the first they deliberately set out to 'foment' sympathy for Germany in England and America, as part of their preparations for the next war. In this they were ably assisted by the much larger army of unconscious propagandists —of ordinary Germans who, when they went abroad or met foreigners in Germany, vigorously presented the German case as they understood it, carrying conviction by their very sincerity.

But even apart from all this, there is no doubt that as the years went by the general assumption in England—it was not, of course, shared by everybody—was that in the early future Germany would be able to settle down with her former enemies on a basis of equality and lasting friendship.

This general approach to the problem was not conditioned to any extent by a theory of racial affinity or by the desire to be linked with Germany against the rest of the world. If an Englishman visiting Germany was told (and he often was) that the two countries ought to have been fighting on the same side instead of against one another he was merely puzzled and shocked. *His* standpoint was that the two countries should not have been fighting at all. Partly, no doubt—any German will say—this was due to the fact that Great Britain had done well for herself in the past and was the outstanding example of a 'satisfied' Power. But chiefly it sprang from the Englishman's realization that war, apart from being evil in itself, was directly contrary to his country's interests. Britain had for over a hundred years depended on international trade for her prosperity and could only be hurt by anything which destroyed the basis of world confidence and peace. Thus it came about that, in the words of a well-known German student, Professor Dibelius: 'England is the solitary Power with a national programme which, while egoistic through and through, at the same time promises to the world something which the world passionately desires: order, progress, and permanent peace.'[1]

The rise of National Socialism represented a severe blow to the growing friendship of Britain for Germany. Not, however, because it led Englishmen to believe that their country was now threatened or that another war was imminent. On the contrary—and paradoxically—its immediate effect on the issue of war or peace was rather in the opposite direction. For the minority of Englishmen, chiefly among the upper classes, who had *not* shared in the general movement towards friendship with Germany and had maintained an attitude more in harmony with that of France, included precisely the people who were most actively and openly apprehensive of the spread of Communism. They accepted the National Socialist claim to be the defenders of Germany against the Bolshevists and they believed that Germany's war ambitions would now be turned eastwards and that Great Britain would be benefited rather than hurt if these ambitions were realized.

But to the majority of Englishmen the National Socialist seizure of power was not interpreted in terms of external power politics at all. It was regarded—and cordially disliked—in terms of its immediate results inside Germany. The destruction of German civil liberties, the oppression of the Jews and the churches and the political opposition parties, the methods of violence of June 30, 1934—all these seemed to the average Englishman the signs of a return to barbarism, and nothing that a German apologist could say in explanation and excuse shook his conviction that they were wrong and disgusting. In spite of this, the forward-looking attitude persisted in England. People were ready to suppose that the National Socialists were simply a brutal and neurotic minority and that the great mass of Germans, though to all appearances supporting them with

[1] Dibelius, *England*, vol. i, p. 117.

enthusiasm, were yet not tarred with their brush. They told themselves, too, that any great national revolution was bound to be accompanied, in its initial stages at least, by some disagreeable manifestations of brutality; there was no reason to assume that they would remain as a permanent characteristic of the German way of life. Above all, they argued, even if England could not feel actively friendly towards a Germany which was apparently ruled by thugs and gangsters, yet she could still hope for a permanent international settlement once Germany's reasonable demands upon the outside world had been fulfilled.

So when Hitler started on his long series of coups, he found in England an attitude of tolerance and compliance which he himself fatally misinterpreted. When he announced his rearmament programme and the reintroduction of conscription, the main reaction in England was that after all the disarmament of Germany had been supposed to be the prelude to a general disarmament within a framework of collective security, and as the latter had not been achieved it seemed only fair to allow the former to go by the board as well; to which was added the hope of the anti-Communists that a strong Germany would be a bulwark against Soviet Russia. The remilitarization of the Rhineland met with a similar reception, though there was in this case a growing feeling of irritation at the manner in which it was done and a recognition that it would not make easier the achievement of friendly relations between Germany and France. Even the annexation of Austria was received with surprisingly little indignation. Though the methods adopted were barbaric, though they showed that Hitler was a man whose word could not be trusted, yet probably the majority of Englishmen were still ready to make excuses for him. After all, they said to themselves, the Austrians are a German people, Hitler himself is one of them and is naturally anxious for the Union; besides, Austria has no future as an isolated nation and when she wanted to join up with Germany in 1931 she was prevented from doing so by France and Italy on power-political grounds. So the end of Austrian independence roused few qualms or regrets among the masses of the British people.

Meanwhile British public opinion had also been moving, slowly but perceptibly, on the question of the colonies. It was not until about 1935 that Hitler showed active interest in the recovery of German colonies, having hitherto rather taken the view, both in his book and in his public utterances, that colonial possessions would be a futile and expensive luxury for Germany.[1] His claims met with a mixed reception in England. On the one hand, there was the inevitable reaction to the effect that 'what we have we hold'. To this was added two further lines of thought: first, that as the former German colonies were administered under mandate from the League of Nations they could only be returned to her by consent of the League as a whole—and Germany had prejudiced her prospects of obtaining that consent by having abruptly left the League a year and a half earlier; and secondly, that the interests of the native populations concerned clearly required that they should not be entrusted to the control of men with the racial theories of the National Socialists—to say nothing of their practical record of violence in their own country. It is easy, but quite mistaken, to dismiss these considerations as mere excuses—as examples of the notorious 'British hypocrisy'. There were large and influential groups in British public opinion who sincerely regarded them as of first-class importance. It was precisely among such people—chiefly but not exclusively idealistic members of the Liberal and Labour parties—that the desire to be fair to Germany was strongest. They had been the leaders in developing the attitude of friendship to Germany during the twenties. The fact that on the colonial issue they were dubious or even opposed was not due to personal self-interest, because the colonies and mandated territories brought no economic advantage to *them*—or at any rate, none of which they were conscious. Even if many Germans chose to believe that they were guilty of self-deception here, yet the fact remains that among the chief opponents to the return of colonies to the Third Reich were precisely the people who had throughout shown themselves to be friends of Germany and advocates of fair and generous treatment to her on all outstanding questions between her and her former enemies.

On the other side, however, many Englishmen felt that there was a strong case in favour of meeting Germany on the colonial issue. Partly this was due once again to the desire to be 'fair' to Germany; as we have seen, it was never taken for granted in England that Germany was to be *permanently* prevented from being a Colonial Power. Partly, too, it arose from an attitude of

[1] See below, p. 155 n.

'appeasement', to use what later came to be almost a technical term in connexion with Anglo-German relations; the attitude, namely, that it was better to acquiesce in minor evils, and even injustices, than to risk the major evil of a second world war. And thirdly, there were those who felt an uneasy conscience about Great Britain's own colonial policy during the preceding decade. Not, indeed, on the ground that the British administration had neglected the interests of the natives. On that issue the British record, though far from spotless, had nothing to fear by a comparison with that of any other Colonial Powers; moreover, it was improving yearly, and those who had the well-being of the natives at heart had every hope of effecting still further substantial advances in this respect during the years to come—a hope which has in fact been justified, as the story of British Colonial Government even during the war years abundantly shows. But the point was that Britain had by now abandoned her traditional 'open-door' policy in the colonial areas. She could no longer say, as she had been able to say before 1914, that the fact that a colonial area was under the British flag involved no economic discrimination against other countries. And therefore in so far as the German claim rested on *economic* grounds the case in favour of it was now, in the thirties, stronger in principle than when that claim had been rejected by the Treaty-makers in 1919.

So in the middle thirties there was a strong disposition in Great Britain to meet the German demand for colonies in a constructive and flexible spirit. On the one hand, many influential people advocated a radical solution of the whole problem along international lines; not merely by making the open-door policy universal but also by applying the mandate system, with all its obligation of trusteeship, to all British and other colonial areas. On the other hand, it was widely agreed that failing such a solution Germany's title to equality of rights in the colonial issue was a strong one provided that her ultimate intentions were really peaceable. As Sir Archibald Sinclair, the leader of the Liberal party, said at the beginning of 1937: 'If Germany were willing to take part in a general settlement, including disarmament, to come back to the League, and to submit all international disputes to third-party judgement, then it would be folly not to meet her by some settlement of the colonial question.'

Nor was this point of view confined to unofficial or non-political quarters. It was adhered to by the Government. Sir Samuel Hoare in 1935 and Mr. Eden in 1936 both declared it to be an object of British policy to see to it that colonial administration should not be carried out in a monopolistic spirit, and at the expense of non-colonial powers. Early in 1937 an International Committee was appointed to study and report on the best and fairest way of meeting the latter's claims; it was also the subject of detailed discussion at the end of that year between the Governments of Britain and France; and Lord Halifax returned from a meeting with Hitler in November, feeling confident that the matter could be dealt with to Germany's as well as Britain's satisfaction and determined to press on towards a final settlement.

Then came the annexation of Austria; the British belief in Hitler's good faith was destroyed, and so too was the disposition to meet Germany on the colonial question, so long as she remained in her existing mood.

6.

With this we come to the summer of 1938 and the Sudetenland coup. The fundamental attitude of Great Britain remained unchanged in principle during this period, but there was a considerable shift in emphasis. As before there was a genuine desire that Germany's reasonable demands should be met. But the demand for the union of the Sudetenland was not universally regarded as 'reasonable', though there were plenty of people prepared to point to the illogicality of the Czechoslovak State as an example of national self-determination, and to the Germanic origin of most Sudetenlanders. Resentment at Hitler's methods was growing, as was the realization of his attitude to treaties and the nature of his technique. The case for a strong Germany as the bulwark against Bolshevism still had its exponents, but it was also becoming apparent that if Hitler went on unchecked he would soon prove a danger to the peace of the world and to the security of Britain herself. Above all, the ordinary Englishman still hoped for peace. So too did his leaders, who knew far better than he did how ill prepared Great Britain was for war.

So while supporting France in her promises of aid to Czechoslovakia, the British Government made a further attempt to bring about a peaceful solution. In August it sent one of its members, Lord Runciman, to Prague as voluntary mediator between the Czechoslovak Government and the Sudetenland minority. After a few weeks Lord Runciman reported in favour of the cession to Germany of areas with a predominantly German-speaking population, while granting complete federal autonomy within the Czechoslovak State to all areas with a narrower Germanic majority. But it was too late. The more the Czechoslovak Government showed its willingness to meet the demands of the National Socialists the more uncompromising the latter became; until at the end of September Hitler presented his ultimatum. War now seemed a certainty. But the British Prime Minister decided to make one last attempt. Stepping into an aeroplane for the first time in his life he flew to Berchtesgaden in the hope that by personal contact with the German leader he might yet save the peace.

What happened then is common knowledge. Mr. Chamberlain did save the peace—for a time, and at the cost of Czechoslovakia. The Munich agreement, signed by the heads of the Governments of Germany, Britain, France, and Italy, without reference to the representatives of Czechoslovakia, gave Hitler all that he had asked for. All that Dr. Beneš got was the promise of a guarantee of its new frontiers by the Four Powers (apart from some minor adjustments in favour of Poland and Hungary) and a loan of 10 million pounds from Great Britain.

When Mr. Chamberlain returned to England from Munich he believed, and so did the vast majority of his fellow-countrymen, that he had deserved well of the world. The shadow of war had lain heavy over Great Britain. Londoners in particular were daily expecting the arrival of hundreds, perhaps thousands, of German bombers, there were no defences, no air-raid shelters, no arrangements for the evacuation of women and children, and all they knew about the German Air Force was that it was incalculably stronger than anything that Britain could put up in the air against it. The first reaction to the Munich settlement was therefore one of overwhelming and indeed hysterical relief. True, after only a few days, more rational considerations came to play a part. People began to wonder whether peace had not been bought too dearly by the betrayal of a peaceful and friendly State. On the whole, however, this doubt was easily stilled. Some took comfort from the fact that it was France, not Britain, who had guaranteed Czechoslovakia, so that the responsibility for the betrayal lay with her; or else they fell back upon the picture of England as a country that was not part of Europe, and need not be entangled in European quarrels. Others, more influenced by National Socialist racial-political theories than they realized, argued that after all the Czechoslovak State had been an anomaly by modern standards, containing as it did a more than 20 per cent. minority of an alien race—to say nothing of the Hungarians and Poles and Ruthenians in its eastern extremity. Still others believed that now at last Germany's demands were within sight of being satisfied. Not so much because Hitler said so—though there still were many Englishmen in high places, incredible as it now seems, who were prepared even in the autumn of 1938 to trust his promises[1]—as because they believed that Hitler was genuinely only interested in peoples of 'German blood', i.e. peoples using the German language, and that when he said on September 26 that he 'did not want any Czechs' that represented a sincere statement of his view. On that assumption all that remained was to make some arrangement with regard to Danzig and any comparable parts of the 'Corridor' and the world might yet avoid a second Great War.[2] Admittedly these further adjustments might involve hardships and even injustices to Poland; but that would at worst be the lesser of two evils, as in the case of Czechoslovakia. As Lord Halifax had said in May (with reference to Mussolini's annexation of Abyssinia), 'where two ideals are in conflict: that of devotion, unflinching but unpractical, to some high purpose, and that of a practical victory for peace, I cannot doubt that the stronger claim is that of peace.'

There were, however, many people whom these arguments did not convince. What they were chiefly conscious of was that Great Britain had acquiesced in an open act of aggression and had bowed before superior force; and they found it difficult to accept—or to forgive—the point of view which treated the Munich settlement as somehow a victory and even a triumph

[1] It is reported that shortly after his return from Munich Mr. Chamberlain had a discussion with a Czech diplomat on the Munich settlement, which he ended with the words: 'The difference between you and me is that you pin your faith on Dr. Beneš: *I* trust Hitler.'
[2] The possibility that on this test Hitler would demand to be given the greater part of Switzerland seems to have been universally overlooked by this school of thought.

instead of recognizing it as at best an unavoidable and deep humiliation, a blow to everything for which Great Britain professed to stand. Added to this current of opinion was a much more widespread awareness that while one might still *hope* to avoid war one could no longer count upon it, and that if a similar crisis should arise again Britain must not be so utterly unprepared as in September 1938. So the British Government announced a rearmament programme, air-raid shelters were constructed and industry was warned of what it would be called upon to do if war were to break out. Even the B.B.C. took its share in the preparations by starting up a tiny news service in German, French, and Italian. . . .

So the winter passed, its comparative tranquillity only being conspicuously disturbed by the savage reprisals inflicted on the Jews in Germany following upon the murder of a German Embassy official in Paris. This episode confirmed the view that the National Socialists were barbarians, increased the feeling that there was something rotten in the German people as a whole that it should allow such a thing, and inexpressibly shocked those who had still been inclined to think of Hitler as a genuinely great man. But otherwise it played little part in the evolution of the British attitude.

But with the spring came the occupation of Czechoslovakia. This had an overwhelming effect. Not merely was it yet another act of aggression carried out in defiance of Hitler's word: it for the first time involved the conquest of an area which by no stretch of the imagination could be called Germanic. Gone was the time when one could make excuses for Hitler on the grounds of his belief in the union of the German race. Now at last it was clear that what he stood for was conquest, naked and unashamed. From that moment onwards the standpoint of British public opinion was that of President Wilson in 1918 after the Treaty of Brest-Litovsk: 'Germany has shown that she believes only in force, therefore it is only by force or the threat of force that she can be held in check.'

Therefore Great Britain gave a public and explicit guarantee to Poland (on which German pressure was now increasing daily) that if she were attacked Britain would come to her aid by force of arms till the aggression had ceased and the wrongs done had been righted.

This guarantee was subsequently quoted by the propagandists

as evidence that Britain was responsible for the war in that she had encouraged the Poles to refuse the German terms when otherwise they might have accepted. It is therefore important to note the relevant dates. The British guarantee to Poland was given on March 31. By that time Poland had already made it completely clear that the German demands were so destructive of her sovereign rights that she was prepared to fight—in however hopeless a war and even if alone—rather than yield to them.

Moreover we must underline the exact significance of the British guarantee to Poland—as of the parallel guarantee to Rumania which was offered by the British Government on the same day. It was not supposed by anybody in England that these assurances could *directly* help the potential victims of German aggression if that aggression were in fact carried out. If Poland (or Rumania) were invaded by Germany, then quite obviously—a glance at the map could confirm this—Britain would be unable to send immediate and effective assistance to the Polish (or Rumanian) army. The point of these guarantees was that they represented a solemn pledge on the part of Great Britain that *if* Germany were to carry out an act of aggression against the countries concerned, then Great Britain would consider herself at war with Germany and would take all possible steps to ensure Germany's defeat. Once that had been achieved, then steps could and would be taken to right any injustices Germany had in the meantime committed.

In other words, Great Britain was in effect saying to Germany, 'If you commit any further act of aggression, then you have to reckon not merely with the country you attack but also with us.' The purpose of the guarantee—and it could hardly have been misunderstood—was to make it clear to Hitler that his one-by-one technique had now reached the limit of its usefulness. The *hope* behind the guarantee was that Germany, even at this last moment, would shrink from precipitating a second world war.

It was a vain hope. Not merely because by that time Hitler was so completely committed to a victory in the Polish issue comparable with his victory less than a year before in the question of the Sudetenland that a withdrawal would have been intolerable to his sense of prestige. Not merely because Hitler knew that some day or other there would be a settlement by force of arms between him and the Western Powers and that the present was as favourable a time from Germany's point of view as he could ever hope for. Though both these points were important, yet the vital thing was that Hitler did not believe that Britain would carry out her undertaking. As Baron Weizsaecker, of the German Foreign Office, told the British Ambassador on July 19, 'Herr Hitler is convinced that England will never fight over Danzig.' And therefore on September 1, having been fully warned of the consequences, he gave the order to the German Army to march across the frontier of Poland, and the Second World War began.

7.

Now, for what is to follow it is vital that we should understand *why* Hitler believed that England would 'never fight over Danzig'.

We may leave aside the possibility that he did not really believe this but thought that he could deal with Britain and France, as well as Poland, then and there. On this question there is room for free speculation. My own view is that while he did think that he could deal with Britain and France as well as Poland if he had to, yet that was not what he intended or wanted. The one-by-one technique was by then well-established in Hitler's mind as a supremely successful way of achieving his ends. If he could have bought off Britain and France (as he bought off Russia), while dealing with Poland, he would then have been in a position either to turn on France and Britain, protected in the rear by the German-Russian pact of August 23, or to turn on Russia relying upon the Anglo-French hostility towards Bolshevism. That is, at the moment, as I say, a matter for conjecture, on which everyone is entitled to his own opinion.

But assuming that Hitler did believe that Britain would not honour her pledge to Poland, the question we have to ask is whether he had any solid ground for that belief.

To some extent it was due to his habit of judging other people by himself. *He* would not have kept his word under similar circumstances; why then should he suppose that England would feel bound by hers?

To some extent, too, it was due to the experiences of a year before. England had in effect committed herself—so Hitler argued—to going to war in defence of Czechoslovakia and had not done so: what ground was there for supposing that she would be more loyal to her commitments in the case of Poland?

But undoubtedly the main factor was a conviction that fundamentally England was weak and degenerate and would never move herself to the rigours of a total war.

Hitler could produce plenty of grounds for that conviction.

There was first the evidence of Ribbentrop, who had been Ambassador in London from 1936 to 1938. Ribbentrop had mixed exclusively with circles friendly to Germany. He had also observed that these circles, though influential, were on important issues opposed to the masses of the English people. Ribbentrop's message was: England is divided in itself, but the people who matter are far too frightened of Bolshevism to want to fight Germany.

Secondly, there was the evidence of the hold of pacifism over the English people. Many respected Englishmen had openly and passionately expressed their conviction that the right attitude to an aggressor was to refuse to fight him and to trust that by one's own self-restraint and meekness one could shame him into abandoning his wicked ways. (Please observe that I am neither attacking nor defending this view, but merely noting that it existed in England in the years before the war and was known to be influential.)

And thirdly, there were the evidences of disunity and internal strife among Englishmen on all sorts of internal and international issues.

In 1933 a meeting of Oxford undergraduates had passed a resolution opposing the idea of fighting 'for King and Country'. In 1935 the country had been rent by the abdication of the King, Edward VIII. In the following years the country had been even more deeply rent by the Spanish Civil War. Did not all these items—and many others too—prove that England was hopelessly divided inside itself and could never present a united front to an external enemy?

The immediate answer to all this is that Hitler was badly served by his agents.

The Oxford resolution was fantastically and culpably misinterpreted by German observers. It was not a resolution in favour of pacifism but an expression of the view of Oxford undergraduates—who on this point undoubtedly represented

the opinion of the Englishman of their generation as a whole—
that the ideal of *national prestige* was not worth fighting for.[1]

The abdication crisis was a matter concerning the country's
attitude to divorce and had no bearing on political issues whatever. In any case, even here the English people was virtually
unanimous—precisely because it felt that the Crown was the
symbol of unity and the reigning monarch must do nothing to
offend the susceptibilities of any large proportion of his subjects.
Had Hitler's agents studied that crisis rightly they would have
reported to him that it was a proof of the fundamental unity,
not of the superficial lack of unity, of the British people.

England's attitude—or attitudes—to the Spanish Civil War
was admittedly a matter of far deeper importance. It was to
Great Britain the first indication of the fact that even an international war may be fundamentally a civil war. That Germany
and Italy were actively supporting General Franco everybody
knew. (Hitler denied it indignantly at the time but admitted it
in so many words a few years later.[2]) That Russia was supporting the Republican Government was equally common property. Therefore the issue in Spain came to be identified in
England with the struggle between those who if it came to it
would support 'Fascism' for the sake of preventing 'Communism', and those who were not frightened of 'Communism' so
long as Britain remained in form and substance a democracy.
The passions aroused by this struggle were indeed so deep-
rooted as to represent a potential threat to Britain's fundamental

---

[1] I was in Oxford at the time as a teacher of economics and can claim to
know what the undergraduates really had in mind.

[2] In his Reichstag speech in June 1937 Hitler declared that Germany,
though hoping for Franco's victory, had no military or political but only
commercial interests in Spain, had introduced an arms embargo, and had
urged that not even 'volunteers' should be allowed to go to Spain for participation in the civil war. A year later official handouts to the German Press
(see, for example, the Vienna edition of the *Völkischer Beobachter* for July 16,
1938) denounced as malicious lies the reports in the London Press of the
presence of German air squadrons in Spain. But on February 23, 1939,
Hitler sent Franco a telegram expressing his pleasure that German 'volunteers' had been able to participate in the struggle against the Republicans,
and four months later (June 6) he told the members of the air units concerned,
the Condor Legion, that his decision to give military aid to Franco was
taken in July 1936, that is to say a year *before* the Reichstag speech quoted
above.

The reaction of most of the Germans of my acquaintance to this last piece
of news was that Germany was entirely within her rights in sending help to
Franco. They had entirely forgotten—some of them vehemently denied—
that Hitler had ever declared Germany to be a non-participant.

unity. If Hitler had been on the Communist instead of on the Fascist side—as well as being Hitler—his hopes might well have been fulfilled. As it was the issue could not have been in any doubt to any German who genuinely understood England. For as soon as it became clear to the British people that he was threatening not merely democracy (in his capacity as a Fascist) but also England (in his capacity as a German) the ranks closed. Some people opposed him only on national grounds, others only on political grounds, still others—almost certainly the great majority—on both. But for whatever reason or combination of reasons, the vital fact was: in the face of the Hitler menace, once it was clearly and unmistakably before their eyes, the British people became completely united. The professional Fascists did not count anyway; the dyed-in-the-wool pacifists, though far more numerous, were still in so small a minority that even after the war had started there was no thought of taking repressive steps against them and they were allowed exemption from military service. And the fact that it was Mr. Chamberlain—the man who in 1938 had in the view of many been willing to sacrifice far too much for the sake of his reputation as a 'man of peace'—that it was Chamberlain who on September 3, 1939, told his fellow-countrymen that he had declared war on Germany and would himself from henceforward do everything in his power to fight 'this evil thing', was the final proof, if proof had been necessary, that in the face of the challenge of the Third Reich internal differences, however fundamental in their own right, were utterly unimportant.

Hitler had indeed been served ill by his agents and advisers when he believed England to be weak and degenerate. But not merely by them. He had also been betrayed by his own propaganda: by the conviction that democracy as such was a weak and inefficient form of government incapable in time of crisis of taking strong action, and by his still more disastrous error of supposing that if a country gives way and is reasonable in the face of threats, that is a proof that it is incapable of making a stand.

Germany believed, then, that England 'would not fight over Danzig', in spite of Mr. Chamberlain's most solemn and specific warnings. Neither did Hitler believe that France would fight over Danzig—would fight at all, for that matter, without

England. In the case of France he had more solid grounds for his belief. The contrasts of economic class and of political philosophy which (as we have seen) were serious in Great Britain, were in France so deep-rooted as to endanger, if not to destroy, the country's unity. The bitterness aroused by the social policy of Blum's Popular Front Government, the instability of the French political structure, the excitability of the French temperament—all this had brought France perilously near to civil strife and anarchy. Would the French forget their internal differences in the face of an external foe? Hitler had good reason for thinking that they would not. His agents were already in close touch with some of the right-wing leaders. A sufficient number of them—not all, indeed, nor even the majority, as it turned out, but a substantial minority—could be relied on when the moment came to place the destruction of the Popular Front and the furtherance of Fascism higher than the safety and honour of France. If they proved unable to prevent France from taking up arms, at least they would see to it that her war effort was half-hearted. Even the possibility of treachery in the field of battle was not excluded. And one good piece of treachery, undertaken at the right moment, would be sufficient to turn the Maginot Line and destroy at a blow the whole structure of French strategy.

About France Hitler had solid grounds for optimism.

Still more could he feel optimistic about the United States. The election of Roosevelt to the Presidency in 1932 had indeed indicated a decline in isolationism. And in subsequent years the United States had taken an increasingly active share in world affairs, striving in particular to cut international trade loose from the network of restrictions and bilateral agreements in which it had since 1931 become entangled. Beyond that, too, dislike of National Socialist methods and suspicion of Germany's ambitions were becoming strong and vocal, especially since the conclusion of the pact with Japan. But that America would *fight* to prevent further German aggression hardly needed consideration. On the contrary she had recently passed legislation directly designed to safeguard her neutrality if a second European war should break out; had been willing to do this at the cost of preventing herself from giving even economic support to the side with which she sympathized. So when President Roosevelt appealed to Germany in April to abstain from further aggression, Hitler felt safe in treating his suggestion with open contempt. There was no force to back it up, and to Hitler force or the threat of force was the only thing that mattered.

What about Russia, then? Here too Germany was on safe ground. Russia was far weaker than Germany, as Hitler well knew. And he knew also how deep were Russian suspicions of the good faith of the Western Powers. No, Russia would not fight. Still, to make assurance doubly sure he would use his well-tried technique and conclude with her a pact of non-aggression. He would break it in due course, at the moment of his own choosing. It would not be a hard job to deal with Russia when the time came. To the traditional Russian inefficiency had now been added the rottenness of Bolshevism; he knew all about Bolshevism: had he not been denouncing it in overwhelmingly convincing speeches for the last twenty years?

So with complete confidence that he had calculated everything in advance Hitler set about making his final preparations.

VI

THE BEGINNING OF THE SECOND WORLD WAR

1.

THE story of the last days of peace are worth telling in some detail.

By the beginning of August, Germany had made it clear that her demands from Poland included not merely the restoration of Danzig to the Reich but also the annexation of the—predominantly Polish inhabited—territory of the 'Corridor'. This last represented an advance on Ribbentrop's earlier demand, for a 'corridor across the corridor'.[1] The Poles had already rejected that demand. Their grounds were clear and cogent. To have agreed to it would have cut Poland off from the sea and would have left her as completely at Germany's mercy as Czechoslovakia had become after the annexation of Austria. The Polish Government knew—as did the whole world—that to give way on this point with Germany in her present mood would have been to ask for destruction. And Poland therefore decided that if she must fight she would fight before being truncated rather than afterwards. Then on March 31 had come the British and French pledges of assistance in the event of German aggression, the British pledge being later (on August 29) formalized into a pact of mutual assistance. Meanwhile the German propaganda machine had been hard at work influencing public opinion against the Poles for alleged and invented atrocities against people of German race, and in Danzig the local National Socialists, on instructions from Berlin and Berchtesgaden, were engaged in systematically flouting the institutions of the Free City as well as persecuting and bullying its Polish inhabitants. Danzig itself was by now a German armed stronghold, filled with members of the Army and the military formations of the Party up to a total of nearly 15,000.

One of the main objects of the fury of the Danzig National Socialists was the Polish customs inspectorate, maintained there under the terms of the Free City's charter. Several

[1] The wider demand was not officially put forward by Hitler or any other National Socialist leader until the last days of August. But it was freely voiced in the Danzig Press in the earlier summer and was indeed a matter of common knowledge.

incidents had occurred in which these officers were prevented from doing their work, and they had on at least three occasions suffered physical violence with loss of life. On July 31 the Polish Government announced that in view of this they would regard various Danzig firms as being outside the Polish tariff system and would subject their exports to Poland to the standard import duties. The Danzig National Socialists as a counter-measure proceeded to inform a number of Polish customs officials that they would no longer be allowed to carry on their work.

On August 4 the Polish Government, acting with the knowledge of the British Minister at Warsaw, addressed a conciliatory letter to the Danzig Senate. It offered to withdraw its tariff measure of five days earlier if the Senate would agree to stop its interference with the work of the inspectorate, but added a warning of the serious consequences which would follow if the Senate made any further arbitrary encroachments on Polish rights.

The Senate agreed to this and for a moment it seemed as though the tension were easing. But in the meantime the Gauleiter of Danzig, Forster (an ignorant and conceited young man, as he was once described to a friend of mine by a high member of the German Government), had flown to Berchtesgaden to discuss the situation with Hitler. Hitler decided to reopen this controversy, which had already been settled between the Senate and the Polish Government; and the method he chose was to have a sharp note sent from Berlin to Warsaw rebuking the Polish Government for their conciliatory communication of August 4. To this the Polish Government replied by pointing out that it had acted entirely within its rights and in the protection of its legal interests, and adding that it would regard any interference with those interests from outside as an act of aggression. Hitler's answer was to move large concentrations of forces up towards the Polish frontier.

On August 22 the British Prime Minister sent a personal letter to Hitler appealing to him to take steps to relax the tension, so that the questions at issue might be settled by peaceful negotiation. This letter was presented to Hitler in Berchtesgaden the next day by the British Ambassador, Sir Nevile Henderson. Later he described the interview as follows:

'Hitler was in a mood of extreme excitability. His language as

regards the Poles and British responsibility for the Polish attitude
was violent, recriminating and exaggerated. Everything was England's fault. She had encouraged the Czechs last year, and she was
now giving a blank cheque to Poland. He preferred war, he said,
when he was fifty to when he was fifty-five or sixty. More than
once he repeated to me that if he had been Chancellor of Germany
in 1914 she would never have lost the war in 1918.'[1]

Hitler's reply to the British Prime Minister's letter was an
uncompromising negative.

But two days later he had a further interview with the
Ambassador and tried once more to employ his old technique.
He was determined, he said, to settle the Polish question in his
own way. But if Britain would break her pledge to Poland, he,
'as a man of great decisions', would pledge himself personally
to the continuance of the British Empire and even guarantee it
German assistance if that should be necessary. He was also
prepared after the Polish issue had been settled to accept 'a
reasonable limitation of armaments', and he declared that he
had no desire to revise the frontiers of western Europe.[2]

In other words, Britain was asked to break a solemn pledge
in return for a postdated cheque drawn in terms of a worthless
and inflated currency. The odd thing about this episode was
only that Hitler should have been so obsessed with the idea of
his own persuasive powers as, to think such an offer worth
making. The promise of German assistance in defence of the
British Empire was an especially bizarre touch, since the only
Powers from which the British Empire was in the remotest
degree threatened were Germany herself and her comrades in
arms, Italy and Japan. Apparently, then, Hitler must have
hoped that the British would take his offer seriously, but that
the more astute Italians and Japanese would not be deceived.
What he to the end failed to grasp was that by the summer of
1939 nobody in the world outside Germany would accept a
Hitler promise, not even if for once it were made sincerely.[3]

The British reply was not confined, however, to a rejection
of this fantastic proposal. It made a series of counter-proposals.
The main ones were the initiation of direct discussions between
the Polish and German Governments and the adoption of
immediate steps to relieve the tension in the matter of the

[1] Henderson, *Failure of a Mission*, p. 257.   [2] Ibid.
[3] See further on this below, pp. 165 f.

treatment of minorities. Great Britain at the same time offered her services, if they should be considered useful, both in negotiating a settlement and in guaranteeing its permanence once it was reached.

Meanwhile other countries too had been doing what they could to persuade Hitler to seek his legitimate ends by peaceful means. President Roosevelt addressed appeals to Hitler and the Polish President urging them not to resort to warfare; he also appealed to the King of Italy to offer his services as a mediator. The King of the Belgians made similar appeals to Germany and Poland in the names of Belgium, the Scandinavian countries, and the Netherlands. The Pope did the same in a personal broadcast from the Vatican. All these efforts were in vain. On August 26 the French Prime Minister sent a letter to Hitler in which he said:

'I owe it to you, I owe it to our two peoples to say that the fate of peace still rests solely in your hands. There is nothing to-day which need prevent any longer the pacific solution of the international crisis with honour and dignity for all peoples if the will for peace exists equally on all sides. I can personally guarantee the readiness which Poland has always shown to have recourse to methods of free conciliation. There is not one of the grievances involved by Germany against Poland which might not be submitted to decision by such methods.'

This letter was presented to Hitler personally by the French Ambassador. The interview lasted for forty minutes. Hitler remained adamant. 'Things have gone too far', he said; and in a letter to the French Prime Minister the next day he added: 'I do not see the possibility of bringing to a pacific solution a Poland who now feels herself inviolable under the protection of her guarantees . . . or of obtaining any result by reasonable means so as to redress a situation which is intolerable for the German people and the German nation.'[1]

But the British proposals for direct discussion could not be pushed aside quite so easily. If they were turned down flatly, then it might be difficult to convince the German people that absolutely everything had been done to achieve a peaceful settlement. On the other hand, they could not be allowed to go through, because if German and Polish representatives met in the presence of third parties and the Poles showed themselves

---

[1] *French Yellow Book*, Documents 254, 261, 267.

conciliatory and accommodating while the Germans rejected all suggestions that fell an iota short of their demands, then once again Germany would have put herself in the wrong. So the German Government decided on two steps: first, to accept the British proposal but interpret it in such a way as to rob it of all reality; and secondly, to accuse Poland of having turned it down.

The first of these plans was carried out as follows. On the day after the submission of the British proposals, that is to say, on August 29, the British Ambassador was summoned to the Reich Chancellery, where he was received by Hitler and Ribbentrop. Hitler handed to him Germany's answer to the British note. It ended with the words, 'the German Government counts on the arrival in Berlin of a Polish Emissary with full powers on the following day, Wednesday, August 30th', in order to receive the settlement proposals which the German Government would in the meanwhile formulate. Now that sentence could only have one meaning. If two parties to a dispute are going to have a genuine discussion with a view to a friendly settlement, then one or other of two procedures will be followed. Either they get in touch with one another to arrange a time and place of meeting convenient to both—and if the matter is very urgent both sides will see to it that the date of meeting is fixed as soon as possible. Or else they start by exchanging letters; one party submitting his proposals to the other and inviting his comments or counter-proposals. The one thing that people do *not* do—if they genuinely desire a friendly settlement—is to *order* their opposite numbers to send a representative with full powers to sign an agreement, neither informing the other side what terms will be put forward nor giving it time to instruct its emissary as to the concessions he may make, and the point at which he must stand firm. If the Hitler–Ribbentrop proposal had been accepted there would have arrived in Berlin the following day an unfortunate Polish official with no idea of what he was going to be asked to sign, no knowledge of how far he could go without breaking faith with his own Government, and only the certainty that he would be bullied and bludgeoned—as Dr. Hacha of Czechoslovakia had been bullied and bludgeoned six months before—till he signed what was put before him. The German proposal was, in fact, an ultimatum to Poland to accept the German terms by midnight on August 30 or accept the consequences.

When the British Ambassador pointed this out, Hitler and

Ribbentrop indignantly protested that it was nothing of the sort. But their subsequent actions belied their words.

For the Polish Government failed to send a plenipotentiary within the time limit laid down. They were, of course, entirely within their rights in this; *unless* the German proposal was intended as an ultimatum they had nothing to fear from looking for a preliminary discussion of the procedure to be adopted in the promised negotiations. At midnight the British Ambassador again called on Ribbentrop. He was able to tell the German Foreign Minister that while Poland had accepted the British proposals without reservation, the German demand seemed to the British Government both unreasonable in itself and wholly incompatible with the spirit of those proposals. And he also appealed to Ribbentrop, on behalf of the British Government, to receive the Polish Ambassador and discuss the best method of procedure. Ribbentrop's reaction to the first of these points was angry abuse; to the second his answer was an equally angry rejection. He then read out at top speed the terms which Germany demanded from Poland as the condition of a settlement. On the previous day Hitler had said in his reply to the British proposals that the German Government would let the British Government know the terms of their demands on Poland if these had been formulated by the time the Polish plenipotentiary had reached Berlin. On the strength of this understanding the British Ambassador asked Ribbentrop for a copy of the document which he had just read out. Ribbentrop refused. And the ground he gave was that the terms were now 'out of date' because it was after midnight and the Polish plenipotentiary had not presented himself. In other words, the German demand of the 29th *was* an ultimatum in Ribbentrop's view and that ultimatum had now expired.

The only thing that need be added is that the Polish Government never received a copy of the German terms. On the 31st the Polish Ambassador received a telegram from Warsaw instructing him to confirm formally Poland's acceptance of the British proposals for direct negotiation. But he was informed at the Wilhelmstrasse that unless he had come with full powers to accept the as yet unrevealed German terms his visit was useless.

Which brings us to the other side of the German procedure: the allegation that Germany had agreed to, but Poland had rejected, the British proposals. This was not merely a distortion of the truth; a moment's thought would have shown that it was a highly unplausible distortion. Even to those who did not know the facts it might have seemed surprising that the Polish Government, having for months laboured with restraint, having made it perfectly clear that though determined to safeguard Poland's legitimate interests it was, above all, anxious for a peaceful and friendly settlement of the issues in dispute, should suddenly turn round and reject a chance of achieving that object. Still more surprising—to anyone who considered the situation objectively—was the German assertion that *Britain* was behind Poland in the alleged rejection of Britain's own proposal. By November 1939 the official National Socialist version of the episode was that Great Britain, as part of a far-reaching plan for the destruction of the Reich, deliberately pretended to Germany that Poland had agreed to direct negotiations when in fact she had turned them down. This would mean, if true, that Britain went out of her way to give Germany the chance of appearing the more reasonable of the two parties to the quarrel and so of justifying herself in the eyes of the world; it hardly squares with the more general allegation that she had for years been systematically engaged in stirring up public opinion against the Reich. In any case, however, the facts were known to Hitler and Ribbentrop. The telegram in which Poland accepted the proposal for direct negotiations was published by the British Government. And any German who, looking back on those days, remembers having been convinced that it was Poland, not Germany, who rejected the British plan, should realize that on this point his leaders quite deliberately and specifically lied to him.[1]

A few days later the propagandists began to give currency to another story, also designed to convince the German people that Poland, not Germany, was responsible for the outbreak of war. This was the story that on September 1 it was the Poles who fired the first shot. Goering, in particular, told the British Ambassador that the invasion of Poland began only after Poland had blown up the bridge over the Vistula at Dirchau. I cannot formally disprove this statement. But even if true, it contributes

---

[1] Needless to say, the German White Book of December 1939, which purported to give all documents relevant to the outbreak of war, contained uo reference to the Polish telegram of August 31.

less than nothing to the establishment of German innocence. In the first place such an act is in itself purely defensive in character: *aggressors* are not likely to destroy the routes over which they will themselves want to pass. Nor, secondly, was it ever suggested that Poland had grandiose plans for an invasion of Germany. She was notoriously preparing to fight only in order to protect her territory. If that is 'aggression', then all resistance to an enemy is aggression—at any rate if the enemy happens to be Germany. On the other hand, Germany's plans for the invasion of Poland were already complete. By August 27 the Army chiefs were becoming impatient at the idea of delay: they feared that bad weather might interfere with the smooth execution of their strategy. It was on that day too—a significant little point—that the war-time rationing system was brought into force for the civilian population. Why exactly Hitler delayed a further five days before giving the order to march must remain at this stage a matter for conjecture.[1] But one thing that is quite certain is that the German Army would *not* have allowed its plans to be held up simply in order to give the Poles a chance of 'firing the first shot'. The war would start when Hitler judged the moment ripe: if a 'first shot' had not by then been fired it could always be invented.

In short the whole attempt to prove Poland guilty of initiating the Second World War is nothing but a series of mis-statements of facts on the one hand and trivial sophistries on the other. Poland's real crime was that she was willing to fight for her national existence. That was the sum total of her 'aggression'. 'Ce pays est trés aggressif; quand on l'attaque il se defend!'

If Hitler had wanted a peaceful settlement with Poland he could have had it. And by choosing the way of peace he would have gained the gratitude, and the honour, of the whole world. Nobody doubted that Germany was strong and could if she wished crush her weaker neighbour by force of arms; the only question was whether she would use her strength in the cause of friendship or of violence. Nobody doubted that the German Army was a potent instrument; the only question was whether the man who wielded that instrument would apply it to building up or to destroying. Germany in 1939 had a God-given oppor-

---

[1] My own guess, for what it is worth, is that Hitler was still hoping that his absurd offer of a 'personal guarantee of the continuance of the British Empire' might succeed in buying Great Britain off.

tunity of displaying that she believed in peace. Under her National Socialist leaders she chose war.

2.

But of course the question of who was the aggressor on September 1, 1939, is only a small item in a much wider issue. As we saw in the last chapter, the propagandists were at work long before the last few days of August trying to establish in the minds of the German people the conviction that if war were to come Germany would be fighting in a righteous cause—in the cause of self-defence and justice. So, too, after the war had started—and particularly when the tide of battle was running against Germany—they repeated and reiterated unwearyingly that the struggle had been 'forced' upon her, that she had been ringed around with foes bent only upon her destruction, that she was herself wholly blameless. Logically this whole type of discussion should have seemed irrelevant and meaningless to believers in National Socialism, who in other contexts were prepared to declare openly that from their point of view the second world war was only a continuation of the first, and who also insisted that in any case questions of justice and morals had no place in the realm of international relations. But the propagandists knew that whatever fanatical Party members might think about such matters they were of immense importance for the ordinary German; he had a deep, at times almost a morbid, desire to justify himself and his acts in his own eyes: he *must* therefore be convinced of his country's innocence if he was to do his best in the national war-effort. To that extent the campaign to prove Germany's guiltlessness was conscious and calculated. propaganda; it was simply a means to an end and had no relation to what the propagandists themselves believed.[1]

Not all the National Socialists were as cold-blooded as this, however. In particular Hitler himself, for all his worship of force, yet gave the impression of being passionately convinced

[1] This, I am sure, was Goebbels's standpoint. When he talked about justice, equality of rights, and the war that had been forced upon Germany he was using language which was designed for his audience and had no real meaning for himself; the passages in his speeches which rang true were far more those in which he gloried in the war as a trial of strength leading to the victory of the stronger, or in which he declared frankly that Germany's war aims were the riches of the East and of the tropics, and that in pursuing such aims the question of morals did not enter, but only that of force.

both of the burning reality of questions of justice and morals and of the truth of his own thesis that in such questions Germany, and he, could claim a wholly clear conscience.

And therefore it is doubly important that we should study the arguments advanced on this issue by the propagandists; not merely as bearing on the history of the years before the war, but also as shedding light on the attitude of Hitler himself—and with him of many of his fellow-countrymen—on the proper relations between Germany and the outside world. The question at issue is that of war guilt, or rather of war responsibility (as we shall see the two concepts are not identical).

The propagandists' case rested on two main theses: that the ensuing war would be a war of *self-defence* and that it would be a *just* war. These two claims are not of course identical. Thus if one country has a just claim to a piece of territory in the possession of another country and having tried unsuccessfully to obtain her rights by peaceful means resorts to warfare, then from her point of view the war may be just—unless we hold that no war can ever be just—but it is certainly not a war of defence. The propagandists were, however, extremely successful in running the two concepts together; thus, as we have just seen, they sometimes used the word 'aggressor' to mean a country which *attacked* (or might at any moment attack) Germany, sometimes to mean a country which set out to deprive her of her 'just' rights. The confusion was useful to them because it helped to create in the minds of their listeners a strong yet vague sense that Germany was being hardly done by and at the same time put difficulties in the way of working out exactly wherein their grievances lay. As we shall see, the grievances if clearly analysed would have proved far less grave and irremediable than it was to the interests of the propagandists to admit.

Let us now take their arguments one by one and see how much truth they contained.

3.

We may start with the doctrine of 'encirclement'. This purported to show that Germany's neighbours were her enemies and therefore that the coming war would be a war of self-defence. It based itself on the series of alliances and agreements made by France with Germany's neighbours on the east and south. And it played a great part in the indignation of the National Socialists when Great Britain entered into her pact of mutual assistance with Poland. But the concept itself is of course far older; it goes back at least as far as the year 1906, when the Chancellor, Prince von Buelow, used it to describe the policy of the Triple Entente. Its purpose at the time was to overcome the opposition to the Big-Navy plans of the Kaiser and Tirpitz. Later on, however, it was applied to the wider purpose of saddling the Entente Powers with the responsibility for the First World War: they had formed an alliance, it was said, for the deliberate purpose of attacking and crushing the German Reich. We need not here discuss whether there was any truth in that allegation. But the use of the term at that time is interesting as an illustration of how what purports to be a simple statement of fact can drift over almost unnoticed into a term of abuse and propaganda. The *fact* was that two countries to the west of Germany and one country to the east of Germany had formed a defensive alliance. To that one could plausibly add that this alliance was directed 'against' Germany in the sense that Germany and her allies represented the group of Powers with which the Entente might one day find itself at war. The *propaganda* came in when this was represented as meaning that the members of the Entente *wanted* war with Germany. As I say, I do not propose to argue whether that conclusion was justified by the facts. The point is that it did not follow simply from the formation of the Triple Entente.

The fundamental fact about encirclement is that it is a matter of geography. In the period with which we are concerned France, Poland, and the Little Entente represented a ring round Germany. But equally after Franco's victory over the Spanish Republicans, Germany, Italy, and Spain represented a ring round France; Germany and Japan formed a ring round Russia; above all—to take the clearest example of all—from 1940 till 1944 National Socialist Germany, Fascist Italy, and Vichy France 'encircled' democratic Switzerland.

Evidently these facts are as they stand wholly neutral. Their political or strategical interpretation depends on the aims and intentions which inspire the formation of these rings.

Now, I hardly think that any German who reflects soberly on the years before the Second World War will find himself believing that the 'encirclement' of Germany at the time was offensive in intention. Germany was not threatened with invasion by land or with bombing from the air. The States concerned had no designs on the territory of the Reich. They did not even try to stop her from becoming strong from a military point of view; they allowed her to rearm, to fortify the Rhineland, to introduce conscription—all of which they could have stopped and certainly would have stopped if they had harboured aggressive designs against Germany.

'Ah', says the propagandist, 'but that was just because they were slack and lazy. When once Germany had become strong they regretted their inaction.' True; they had every reason to regret their inaction afterwards, when it was too late. But the reason for that regret was not the fact of Germany's strength but the uses to which they began to foresee that that strength would be put. Once it became clear that Germany proposed to seize territory from neighbouring States by force or the threat of force the picture changed fundamentally. The Powers concerned *did* then start thinking in terms of a strategical, as opposed to a purely geographical, encirclement. But that was not because they had aggressive intentions towards Germany, but because they felt themselves threatened by Germany. They were anxious to defend their own territory from attack.

' "Their own territory", indeed,' retorts the propagandist; 'the purpose of the encirclement policy was deliberately to prevent Germany from recovering territory which belonged to her and of which she had been robbed by the Treaty of Versailles.' But in saying that he has abandoned the original basis on which the encirclement doctrine was advanced. He is now objecting to the agreements and alliances among Germany's neighbours, on the ground that they were designed to deprive her of her just rights, not on the ground that they were designed to subject her to armed attack. The argument has shifted from the realm of 'defence' to that of 'justice'.

It is worth while illustrating this point with special reference to the British guarantee to Poland. That guarantee was given on March 21. Between that date and the end of August it was constantly asserted in Germany that it was not merely a barefaced piece of 'encirclement' but also that it was directly responsible for Poland's intransigence.[1] Now an immediate answer to

[1] See, for example, the account of the interview between Hitler and the

this complaint, as the narrative of events given in the last chapter shows (p. 118), is that the Poles had made clear their determination not to accede to the German demands at the beginning of the year—that is to say, well before they had any ground for expecting a British guarantee. Moreover, it was obvious to them, as to everybody else, that in the absence of an agreement with Russia Great Britain could do nothing to prevent Poland from being overrun if the German Army were to invade. So there is no ground for believing that the British guarantee made any difference whatever to Poland's attitude. But suppose that it was as important as Hitler claimed; suppose, for instance, that but for the guarantee he could have succeeded, by bullying, threatening, and nerve war, in breaking down Poland's resistance: what follows from that? Not, certainly, that Britain and Poland either together or separately were planning to attack or invade the Reich, or in any way to interfere with its internal affairs; but simply that Britain considered the demands on Poland to be unreasonable (a fact which was abundantly clear in any case) and saw in a guarantee to Poland a possible method of preventing their fulfilment. Whether one holds Britain justified in giving her guarantee or not depends entirely upon one's view of the justice of these demands.

We shall come back to that question in a moment. Meanwhile, our conclusion is that the doctrine of 'encirclement' contributes nothing to the propagandists' case which will stand up to analysis. All that is left of it is that *if* Germany's territorial claims on her neighbours were in themselves moderate and reasonable, then action taken by other nations—whether by encirclement *or in any other way*—to prevent the satisfaction of those claims was prima facie unjust. A war undertaken to enforce them might then be called a just war. What we cannot say is that it would be a war of self-defence.[1]

British Ambassador on August 23 (pp. 126 f.) and the quotation from his letter to the French Prime Minister four days later (p. 128).

[1] This may sound to some like a mere debating point—fair, perhaps, as far as it goes, but proving nothing of substance. It is, however, of considerable importance in considering the propagandists' case as a whole. That case appears to consist of a large number of different points, each one supplementing and strengthening the others. By showing that some of these points are simply variations on others, or depend entirely upon others for any validity they may have, one can cut away a vast tangle of empty rhetoric and can thus hope to discover where the real substance of the propagandists' arguments is to be found.

4.

The next argument to be considered concerns the position of
people of Germanic origin living as racial minorities outside the
territory of the Reich. The propagandists made immense play
with the sufferings of such people—first in Czechoslovakia and
then in Poland. (I have not come across any reference whatever
in National Socialist speeches during this period to the position
of the German-speaking population of the South Tyrol. Perhaps
that was due to come later.)

Here, again, the element of 'justice' and the element of 'self-
defence' were closely and skilfully intertwined, to the confusion
of clear thinking. On the one hand it was argued, or implied,
that as these were 'Germans' who needed to be protected against
oppression and cruelty, a war conducted with that end in view
would be essentially a 'defensive' war. On the other hand, the
fact that the persons concerned were claimed as Germans was
used as overwhelming proof of the 'justice' of the claim to have
the territories they inhabited ceded to the Reich.

Now there is no doubt that the greater part—I do not say the
whole—of the problem of the German minorities in Czechoslovakia and Poland was directly due to National Socialist policy
and propaganda. First they deliberately organized cells of agitation in the areas concerned. These were built up into National
Socialist parties, the members of whom deliberately set out to
get themselves into trouble with the Governments and the non-
German majorities of the countries to which they belonged. If
the authorities took action against them—as they were bound
to do at times, if only for the sake of preserving order—then that
was at once trumpeted abroad as a 'persecution' of people of
German race. If, as sometimes also happened, the non-German
population were provoked into violent action against the trouble-
makers, so much the better; the evidence of persecution was
that much stronger and at the same time the sympathy of the
outside world would veer round towards the German minority.
Meanwhile, the ordinary German-speaking citizen of these
countries would find himself caught up in the whirlpool of
agitation and controversy. Flattered at finding himself a topic
of international importance, delighted to be told that he was
something he had not thought of before, namely a member of
an ill-treated minority, he would make the most of any little

trouble he might have had with the authorities, or any friction between him and his non-German neighbours, and that too would go to swell the list of 'incidents' which according to the propagandists cried out for immediate and radical action.[1]

But the National Socialists were not content with stirring up and magnifying trouble inside the areas they wished to claim for the Reich. In addition they resorted to the manufacturing of evidence and direct lying. For example, during the summer of 1938, the German Press made much of the fact that a stream of Sudeten Germans had crossed the frontier 'to escape from Czech persecution'. Some of these refugees gave terrible stories to reporters of their sufferings. What was not published was that the Sudetenland National Socialist Party had sent round instructions to every German village to select and send off to Germany a stipulated number of its inhabitants as refugees. In one case known to me the wife of the local miller was among those selected. She was put in a settlement in a village not far from Berlin, but soon became discontented. A friend of mine who lived in the neighbourhood met her and to him she poured out her complaints. 'I've been here for over a month now: they said I would not have to stay longer than a fortnight.' 'Who said so?' my friend asked. 'Why, the peasants' leader', was the answer; 'he told me I had to come, but I want to go back to my husband.' 'Why wasn't he sent with you?' '*He* couldn't leave: he's got the mill to look after.'

A similar technique was no doubt employed a year later in the case of the German-speaking minority in Poland, though I have no direct evidence of this. But there the chief emphasis was on other, simpler, methods. The first was that of exaggeration. Thus, in Hitler's letter of August 27 to the French Prime

[1] An example of what I mean is provided by the following story. In a Sudetenland village, a place to which visitors used to come, for it was a picturesque place, there was a little old-fashioned German inn, the proprietor of which made a good livelihood from his trade. One day a syndicate decided to build a large modern hotel in that village. And the result was a sad decline in the profits of the German innkeeper. The syndicate was supposed to be owned by Czechs, though nobody knew this for certain. This episode was cited to me in all seriousness and with genuine indignation by a Berlin bank official (who had had it himself from the innkeeper) as an example of the shocking persecution of the Sudeten Germans by the Czechs. At the time I was merely amused that my acquaintance should show such a lack of a sense of proportion. But his attitude was symptomatic, as was that of the innkeeper. The latter had become a self-conscious member of an 'ill-treated German minority'. The former was a laboratory specimen of what National Socialism could do to even an educated German citizen.

Minister, it is stated that the number of Germans in Poland was 'nearly two millions'. In fact the number was fewer than one million—no more than the number of Poles in Germany, as the German Ambassador to Poland admitted to the French Ambassador the following day.[1] A similar demonstrable exaggeration was contained in Hitler's estimate of the number of German 'refugees' from Poland during the first half of 1939. The main emphasis, however, was on straight lying. Most Germans will still remember how during these months their newspapers were full of atrocity stories—how in this or that town in the Corridor so and so many hundred Germans had been evicted from their homes, arrested, robbed, or murdered by the Poles. If even a fraction of these stories were true, then there was an overwhelming case for taking action—*appropriate* action. The first and most obvious step to take, *if* Germany had simply been concerned to protect the lives and property of people of German race, and was still anxious to maintain friendly relations with Poland, would have been for the German Government to take the matter up with the Polish Government, protesting as vigorously as it felt disposed, but at the same time giving chapter and verse of the incidents complained about. In fact it never did that. It could not because the incidents had never taken place. On July 15 the German Ambassador in Warsaw told his French colleague that 'while he had cause to complain of certain *administrative* measures taken by the Polish authorities against the Germans he had not had to complain of acts of any other kind for some time past'.[2] And the following passage is worth quoting from a letter sent by the French Ambassador to his Government in Paris on August 28: 'the ill-treatment, murders, &c., of which the Poles are accused by Chancellor Hitler are sheer calumnies. It is impossible for Germans to be killed on the outskirts of Danzig or at Bielsko without the knowledge of the French who live in these districts. Moreover, it should be pointed out that the Germans have not mentioned any definite facts, names or dates.'[3]

As for the situation in Danzig—allegedly so intolerable for the ordinary German citizen there—it is only necessary to point out that towards the end of July the local National Socialist leader, Forster, on his return from an interview with Hitler, told the

---

[1] *French Yellow Book*, Document 282.
[2] Ibid., Document 275.   [3] Ibid., Document 276.

acting British Consul that the Danzig question could, if necessary, wait for a year or more.[1]

There is, in short, overwhelming evidence that the atrocity campaigns against the Czechs in 1938 and the Poles in 1939 were from start to finish the work of National Socialists, either in the areas concerned or else in the Propaganda Ministry or the Office for Germans Abroad in Berlin. That there may have been occasions on which Germans in the countries concerned suffered violence at the hands of their non-German neighbours is probable. As I have said, their conduct was deliberately designed to provoke such violence and not every individual Pole could be expected to possess the almost superhuman self-restraint displayed by the Polish Government during the first eight months of 1939. After the war had started the situation of course changed. Though I do not for a moment credit the figures published in the German Press during the autumn about the 'massacres' in Bromberg and other towns—if only because those figures themselves varied up and down from day to day and from paper to paper—yet it is not to be supposed that the German populations in towns behind the Polish front line, representing as they did an immense 'fifth column', escaped without loss of life or liberty. But that is not part of the issue we are here considering—which is the truth, or falsehood, of the propagandists' allegation that the campaign against Poland was forced upon Germany by the need to defend her blood-brothers from an already existing reign of terror of unexampled severity. That allegation will not stand up to a moment's objective scrutiny. Apart from the fact that (as we have seen) there is no genuine evidence in support of it and that plenty of the supposed evidence can be shown to be false or manufactured, there are three further points of a more general nature which need to be mentioned, and I invite any German who still wonders whether, after all, the propagandists may not on this point have been telling the truth, to consider them carefully.

First, is it likely that Poland or Czechoslovakia would run a systematic campaign of atrocities against citizens of German blood just at the time when they were faced with an imminent threat from Germany to their national sovereignty and independence and were trying by all means in their power to settle the issues in dispute peacefully?

[1] British Blue Book of Sept. 3, 1939, p. 78.

Secondly, how is the fact to be explained that in both cases the stream of atrocity stories flowed into the offices of German newspapers and to the German Broadcasting Company just at the time when Hitler's interest was turning towards the countries in question? There were no atrocity stories from the Sudetenland before the spring of 1938; no atrocity stories from the Polish 'Corridor' till the spring of 1939. Did the Governments of Czechoslovakia and Poland, having hitherto been at the least not spectacularly oppressive to their German minorities before, deliberately begin to commit atrocities *just* at the moment when they saw that Hitler had disposed of the last victim of his one-by-one technique and was now ready to apply it to them? Or are we to suppose that the atrocities were going on all the time, but that Hitler had failed to hear about them or was callous enough not to give them publicity?

And thirdly, from the point of view of the German Government the atrocity stories were invaluable propaganda material and were skilfully used for uniting the majority of Germans in support of its policy. In view, then, of the National Socialist doctrine as to the relation between propaganda and truth, as expounded in certain world-famous passages from *Mein Kampf*, is there any ground whatever for supposing that because the German Press was at the time full of atrocity stories, therefore the atrocities described took place?

Here, too, it appears, the 'self-defence' argument breaks down completely. We are still, however, left with the argument from 'justice'—the doctrine that if an area contains a large proportion of German-speaking inhabitants it is unjust that it should not be a part of the Reich.

This issue raises the whole complex question of National Socialist racial theories and cannot be given the treatment due to it here. But the following points may be summarily noticed.

First, the doctrine rests on the assumption—or rather on the explicitly stated thesis—that if two groups of people belong to the same race they should also belong to the same nation. Now, this is not merely not a self-evident truth, it has never formed a part of currently accepted political philosophy except in Germany, and even there it is a doctrine of comparatively recent growth. As the basis of a far-reaching foreign policy it dates from the rise of National Socialism. History is full of examples of races which have been divided among two or more nations, and of nations which have comprised two or more races. To take present-day examples only, let us reflect over how many 'nations' the Spanish 'race' is spread; or how many 'races' are included within the Russian 'nation'. Within the British Isles there are to-day two independent sovereign States—the United Kingdom and Eire. There are also at least two 'races'—the 'Anglo-Saxons' and the 'Celts'—at least as distinct from one another ethnologically as are the Germans from the French. But the two lines of demarcation do not coincide. On the contrary a large proportion of 'Celts' live within the United Kingdom—namely in the Highlands of Scotland and in Wales. These peoples do not feel themselves to belong to the same 'nation' as the people of Eire. Nor does the latter claim them for herself: on the contrary her expressed and open ambition is to absorb the area of Northern Ireland, at present part of the United Kingdom, which contains a large proportion of Protestant 'Anglo-Saxons'.

Secondly, the presence of large numbers of people of German origin in the Sudetenland has been due, as is well known, to a long process of infiltration across the mountains from Bavaria, Saxony, and Silesia, and of migration from Austria. Similarly, the German minorities in the Polish 'Corridor' are made up of the descendants of emigrants and settlers—to say nothing of soldiers of fortune—who at different times during the last seven centuries 'pushed eastwards' and acquired new homes in the midst of a predominantly Slav population.[1] In both cases the incomers were people who increasingly left their former homes in purely · German States and in fact 'emigrated'. It may be rejoined that the fact that they did so proved Germany's need of a larger territory than she at the relevant periods possessed. The merits of this contention will be examined in a moment when we come to the doctrine of the German 'living space'. The point here is simply that the Sudetenland was never historically a part of Germany, and the Polish province of

---

[1] It is perhaps hardly necessary to emphasize that anybody who believes the 'Corridor' to have been created by the Treaty of Versailles simply as a means of giving Poland an outlet to the sea and to be essentially a German-inhabited area is ignorant of the facts. It is a Polish area, but one with a large German minority—almost exactly as large as the Polish minority allocated by the Treaty of Versailles to Germany.

Pomerania only became so by deliberate acts of conquest of an alien people on the part of Prussia.

Thirdly, many Germans emigrated not owing to economic necessity but to escape from political and religious oppression. In particular they went in large numbers to the United States during the nineteenth century as 'protestants for freedom', to use the phrase of a distinguished American of German descent, Mr. Wendell Willkie. They left Germany because they no longer wanted to belong to the German nation. But that did not mean that they renounced their German race or popular traditions; on the contrary, it is well known that there are many communities in the United States in which these traditions are vigorously and obstinately kept alive. If such people are in principle to be included within the German *nation*, then they will be so included contrary to their own wishes. So far as they are concerned the identification of race with nation, far from being self-evidently reasonable, constitutes a direct threat of force and violence, utterly opposed to the principle of 'self-determination', to which the propagandists so frequently appeal in connexion with German minorities outside the Reich.

In fact, of course, the National Socialists never openly demanded the cession of western Pennsylvania and other German-inhabited areas of the United States, and when in 1941 President Roosevelt announced the discovery of a secret plan showing how after Germany had subjugated Europe she could get to work on the conquest of the American continents Hitler angrily brushed it aside (using, as it happens, almost exactly the same language as he had used in 1934, when asked whether he intended to annex Austria). And in truth the idea that Germany should annex large portions of the United States because of the racial origin of their inhabitants is absurd—patently so. Yet it is a logical and inescapable consequence of the doctrine which sets out to identify 'race' with 'nationality'.[1]

And here we come to the last and really fundamental point.

---

[1] Both Hitler and, still more, Mussolini used language suggesting that they regarded themselves as the rightful leaders of the many millions of American citizens of German and Italian descent. Not merely that, but a minority of these American citizens were prepared to work on Hitler's behalf and set up at least the cadre of a National Socialist organization—whether willingly because they had been infected by National Socialist doctrine or under the threat of what would happen to their relatives in Germany if they refused. But these activities lie outside the scope of our present argument.

The essential fact about all the areas in which there are German minorities is that they are inhabited by *mixed* populations. Partly this is a matter of (so to speak) spatial interspersion: predominantly German towns set in the middle of a predominantly non-German country-side, streets in a given town, or even houses in a given street, occupied alternately by German and non-German inhabitants. Partly it is a matter of racial fusion through intermarriage. In either case it intolerably complicates the simple scheme which the propagandists wish to impose.

The problems raised by interspersion are in the first instance simply administrative. The areas concerned have to be organized and run by a central authority of some kind, presumably a sovereign State. (Arrangements can be made for a condominium of some kind between the nations immediately concerned but are most unlikely to be satisfactory.) Until the First World War the universal assumption and practice was that the mixed-population areas would come within the territory of the stronger of the States interested. In the Treaty of Versailles this assumption was abandoned. Under the influence of President Wilson's doctrine of self-determination the Treaty-makers endeavoured to substitute the principle that the control should be decided by the majority vote of its inhabitants. This principle was not, indeed, held to have over-riding authority in all cases. On the contrary, the Treaty-makers recognized that it must on occasion be subordinated to considerations of security and even of economic or geographical necessity. But they held the view that, *unless there were compelling reasons to the contrary*, any area should belong to that State to which the majority of its inhabitants had the closest affiliations.[1]

That solution, however, automatically meant that the minority of these inhabitants had a prima facie excuse for feeling that they were being badly treated. And so the minority problem emerged—not, be it noted, because the Treaty did its work badly, but on the contrary because it tried to consider the wishes of the inhabitants instead of settling things in terms of political might.

Perhaps the Treaty was less careful than it should have been to safeguard the rights of these minorities; certainly it failed

---

[1] This is, of course, a simplification of the problem in that it does not raise the issue of how an 'area' was defined. But it fairly describes the spirit in which the Treaty-makers attempted to find a solution (cf. above, pp. 48 f.).

(as we have seen) to understand the economic aspects of the problems involved. And there is no doubt that in various ways those citizens of the newly created States of Czechoslovakia and Poland who regarded themselves as being Germans, rather than Czechs or Poles, suffered from various political disadvantages from their minority position—most of them arising out of the language problem; disadvantages precisely comparable with those suffered by the inhabitants of Silesia and Pomerania who felt themselves to be Poles rather than Germans.

But in any case the problem was insoluble in racial terms. Short of the drastic expedient of conducting wholesale transfers and exchanges of populations, there were *bound* to be minorities in the mixed-population areas.

And therefore when the National Socialists demanded the cession of the Corridor to Germany they were not basing their case on racial considerations as understood by the Treaty-makers. On the contrary, they were proposing a return to the pre-Versailles view; the view that Germany was entitled to the area in question—even though its inhabitants were predominantly non-Germanic—simply because Germany was in their estimation a 'greater' nation than Poland, and because it was an essential part of their creed that in the presence of the German people 'inferior' races had no rights whatever. We are not at the moment concerned to analyse or appraise this view; that will come later. But it is vital to recognize that there was no case on 'racial' grounds for the National Socialists' demands on Poland except on the assumption that the well-being of a German was as such more important than the well-being of a Pole—or, indeed, of several Poles. The argument from 'racial justice', in short, dissolves on examination into an assertion of the overriding rights of the German master race.

In the Sudetenland the situation was the same in essentials, though with an important variation of emphasis. Here the chief problem from the point of view of the National Socialist racial theorist was rather more that of fusion than of interspersion. At the end of the eighteenth century the fringes of Bohemia— where Germans and Austrians had lived side by side with Czechs for eight centuries, sometimes quarrelling, often at peace —became the industrial workshop of the Austro-Hungarian Empire. The opening up of factories attracted many Czech peasants into what had hitherto been mainly German towns.

To some extent these retained their separate identity, in which case the problem was essentially that discussed above in connexion with Poland. But to a large extent they lost their separate identity *as races*.

That did not mean, of course, that the distinction between 'Germans' and 'Czechs' was ceasing to exist. Obviously it was not; indeed, with the collapse of the Austro-Hungarian Empire it became sharper than ever. But it was a distinction based on national affiliations as a whole, and many factors besides ancestry came in to decide where any given individual's national affiliations would lie: language, religion, social position, type of work, political leanings, even personal temperament.[1]

In other words, the 'racial' test is of no use whatever in determining whether an area of mixed populations should be assigned to one country or to another. The National Socialists in preaching 'racial purity' were guilty of a twofold error: first in thinking —or implying that they thought—that it was a practical test at all: a consideration of the Wends in the Spreewald and the Masurians in East Prussia (to speak only of modern times) would have shown them that even areas of allegedly purely German populations might contain large admixtures of non-Germans; and secondly in confusing 'race' with 'nationality', and supposing that they had proved that a particular area naturally formed part of Germany's heritage if the peoples in that area— or any large proportion of them—had German names or used German as their language.

A realistic approach to the problem of the German minorities would have shown that it did not admit of a solution that would be both simple and just. If the National Socialists had really been concerned with a peaceful settlement they would have

[1] We need not discuss these matters in detail. It is, however, perhaps worth pointing out in view of the propagandists' tendency to regard language as conclusive evidence of racial origin that in bilingual areas such as these the preference for one language over the other tends to be determined far more by education and social contacts than by ancestry. To take one example, the mother of the first President of Czechoslovakia, Masaryk, though coming of a Czech family, spoke German by upbringing and had to learn her native language after she was grown up.

It should be added that the policy of Germany, from the time of Frederick the Great up till 1914, was deliberately to encourage, and even impose, German as the language to be used by those of Polish race within the frontiers of the Reich. Even to-day there must be many people living east of the Oder who are of wholly or predominantly Slav ancestry but speak nothing but German.

dropped their rodomontades about racial purity and German blood, and would have set to work to deal with any concrete subjects of dispute by negotiation and discussion. At one time it looked as though Hitler realized this. In May 1935 he told an American interviewer that 'We have, of course, a fellow-feeling with those of our own blood beyond our frontiers; but what profit would there be in regaining a few hundred thousand souls at the cost of the slaughter of millions?' An admirable and wise sentiment. What a pity that Hitler did not mean it.

5.

We come now to a series of propaganda themes which made no real pretence of arguing that the coming war would be a war of self-defence, but aimed rather at *justifying* the purposes for which it would be fought—though even here the confusion between 'defence' and 'just claims' was sometimes maintained by speaking of the purposes in question as amounting to 'the defence of Germany's vital interests'. They centre round two main concepts: that of Living Space and that of Equality of Rights. But it is not easy to sort out the arguments tidily under these two heads. Thus the case for the return of colonies was primarily a demand for equal rights with other Great Powers, but was often presented in the form of a claim to (colonial) living space; conversely the living-space argument might be stated absolutely as a claim for as much territory as Germany from her own point of view required; or it might be stated relatively as a claim for as much territory, in proportion to her population, as other nations—i.e. in the form of a demand for *equality of rights* in respect of living space.

With this proviso in mind let us start with the problem of 'Living Space'.

On April 28 1939 Hitler declared in the Reichstag: 'According to all common sense, logic, and all principles of a general human and of a higher justice, nay even according to the laws of a Divine Will, all nations ought to have an equal share in the goods of this world.' What exactly does this mean?

What it *says*, if taken literally, is that each of seventy-two self-governing States of the world should have exactly one-seventy-secondth of the world's total resources. That would, however, give Haiti or Liberia as much as Germany, would give

Germany far less than she at present possesses, and is clearly not what Hitler has in mind.

Does it, then, mean that the world's goods should be distributed among the nations in proportion to the size of their populations? In this form the proposal might commend itself to the common sense of at least the poorer half of the world's inhabitants. But it is still not what Hitler means; for if it were, then once again Germany would suffer. Her population at the time when he was speaking constituted some 4 per cent. of the total population of the world as a whole, whereas her wealth, whether interpreted as her national capital or her national income, was certainly more than 4 per cent.—perhaps 6 or 7 per cent.—of the wealth of the world as a whole.

No, from other statements made by Hitler and his followers it is clear that what he is demanding is equality (in proportion to population) not of goods, but of *territory*. He is saying that the *density* of population should be the same throughout the world.

This is, however, by no means a self-evident proposition. In the first place, any such arrangement would be patently unjust unless it also took into account differences in fertility and in mineral wealth. If, for instance, France had ceded the Central Sahara to Germany the result would have been a sharp increase in the 'density of population' of the French Empire and a sharp decrease in that of the German Empire, but there would have been little loss to France or gain to Germany, and the National Socialists would not have regarded the gift as a major contribution to the satisfaction of their living-space demands. What Germany demanded was, not land, but *useful* land.

The propagandists did not attempt to conceal this, of course; on the contrary, in other contexts they actively insisted on it. But for the purposes of the living-space doctrine they continued to talk as though the proportion between area and population were all that mattered. Thus in the speech from which I have just quoted Hitler went on to say: 'It should not happen that one nation'—viz. America—'claims so much living space that it cannot get along when there are not even 15 inhabitants to the square kilometre, while others are forced to maintain 140, 150, or even 200 in the same area.' We hardly need stop to point out that in this passage Hitler both understates (slightly) the density of population of the United States and overstates (grossly) the density of population elsewhere—since there is no nation in the world with an overall density exceeding 135 per square kilometre, the figure for Germany.[1] The point is rather that by speaking in these simple and dramatic arithmetical terms the propagandists were able greatly to exaggerate the extent to which Germany was at a disadvantage as compared with other countries. Germany contains $3\frac{1}{2}$ per cent. of the world's population, they argued, and less than half of 1 per cent. of the world's land area; therefore by rights Germany should have more than seven times the land that she in fact possesses—and if their audiences got the impression that the extra land which one day would come to them, when justice was done, would consist entirely of rich agricultural land and plantations teeming with tropical fruits, then so much the better!

And this brings us to a further point of some importance. The propagandists were fond of saying, or implying, that the territory of Germany was not merely small in area but also poor in nature. Here again they grossly exaggerated. A good deal of her agricultural land is indeed less naturally fertile than that of (for example) many parts of England or France—though it is far more fertile than Italy or Greece, or vast stretches of the steppes and tundra of Russia. In respect of mineral resources, on the other hand, Germany, like England, is endowed with resources well above the average. For that reason, it was natural that Germany, again like England, should have become an *industrial* country—a country with a larger proportion of factory workers to land workers than one finds in the world as a whole. Hitler, it is true, regarded this as a bad thing; his demand for more living space was based in *Mein Kampf* precisely on the desire to achieve a 'healthier balance' between industry and agriculture, by increasing the numbers of the German peasant class. But whatever we may think of the merits of this programme—certainly it appealed to many Germans who were not National Socialists, as it to-day appeals to many people in other

[1] The density of population, *in the motherlands only*, of Belgium, Holland, England, Japan, and Italy are higher than this figure. But the addition of these countries' colonial areas, with their inhabitants, brings the figure in every case down to well below the German level. As a rule this point formed one of the main planks in the propagandists' case and it is curious that Hitler should have made such a slip. The explanation is, no doubt, that in April 1939 (as in *Mein Kampf*) he was thinking far more of the increase of Germany's living space at the expense of her eastern neighbours than of the acquisition of colonies. See below on this, p. 155 and n.

countries besides Germany—it must be stressed that the in-
dustrialization of Germany was in the circumstances of the
nineteenth century an inevitable result of her advantages in
respect of mineral resources. What would have happened if she
had *not* possessed this mineral wealth I do not know. Certainly
her standard of living would have been far lower, almost certainly emigration to the New World would have taken place on
a far larger scale while the door was still open, possibly the
threat of world wars for more living space would have manifested itself earlier. As it was, Germany by becoming a leading
industrial country was able (once again like England) to support
—and indeed required—a relatively high density of population.

But none of this in the least implies that Germany (or Britain)
is *over*-populated. The concept of over-population is usually
taken to mean a population too large to provide the highest possible standard of life for the individuals composing it. The test
of whether a given area is or is not over-populated would be to
effect a sudden decrease in the number of its inhabitants and
see whether, when all the necessary adjustments in its economic
and social life had been carried through, the remaining citizens
were better off than before or not. Now it is by no means certain
that if Germany's population in 1939 instead of being 75 millions
had been, say, 50 millions the average income per head would
have been higher. For while the amount of land and natural
resources per head would have been greater, the amount of
labour power available for exploiting that wealth would have
been less and there would have been less scope for the economic
division of labour and industrial specialization on which the
mass production of consumption goods so largely depends.
And it is entirely possible that the loss in this latter respect
would more than counterbalance the gain in respect of area per
head. I do not of course say that this result would be *certain*:
economists have not yet succeeded in devising methods for veri-
fying the point, and in my view it is unlikely that they ever will.
But equally there is no evidence to disprove it, and we must
therefore return a completely open verdict on the question of
whether or not Germany was 'over-populated' in the proper
sense of that term.

Nor on a more short-run, practical point of view did Germany
show any signs of being burdened with an excessive population
during those years. The first thing to do in that case would have

been to ban all foreigners from working in German factories and to see to it that only those people were allowed to live and work in Germany who were real members of the German community. In fact precisely the opposite policy was adopted. The National Socialists encouraged and almost compelled the immigration of foreign workers; Germans who were working abroad were summoned back; Germans who wished to emigrate were refused passports. In fact the whole attitude of the National Socialists was to regard a large population as an asset and a source of strength; to be worried by a shortage of labour, rather than by a shortage of the land and raw materials on which that labour might work. Hence the opening words of the proclamation on the Food Production Campaign in 1934: 'Germany is poor in space, *but Germany is rich in population* and rich enough in all resources to ensure the feeding of her people.' Hence too the hopes of the National Socialists that in the years to come the German population would increase by leaps and bounds, and the practical measures taken to secure that end. On this matter, indeed, the National Socialists were utterly out of touch with reality. Hitler in *Mein Kampf* declared that in a century's time the total number of Germans in Europe would be 250 millions;[1] and Goebbels in 1939 based an attack on the Western Powers for their attitude to Germany's claims on the proposition that after fifty years 'the 80 million Germans will be 130 million'. A glance at the German Government's own official publications would have shown them that these figures were wildly exaggerated. In 1938 the Reich Statistical Office published a calculation showing the probable trend of the German (including the Austrian) population, from which it appeared that the total figure would reach Goebbels's *present* claim of 80 millions by 1960, would remain at about that figure for some twenty years, and would then begin gradually to decline. These calculations took full account of the effects of the National Socialist campaign for the encouragement of marriages and large families, they assumed that this campaign would yield even fuller results in the future, and they also reckoned on an early reduction in the infant mortality rate by nearly a half, besides making no allowance for the increase in adult mortality rates owing to war.[2]

[1] p. 767.
[2] *Wirtschaft und Statistik*, 1938, pp. 971–5. It is perhaps worth remarking

But the propagandists *wanted* to believe their fantastic stories of the future growth in Germany's population, not merely because they wanted Germany to become the strongest nation in the world, but also because the larger the number of Germans, the more convincing, they felt, was their case for an increased living space. Seen in this light the living-space doctrine took on a wholly new aspect—from the point of view of other nations a much more sinister aspect. It was no longer a claim for relief from the burden of an existing over-density of population; it was rather a warning that Germany intended to elbow herself into a more dominant position among the world's Great Powers.

In another way too the doctrine showed chameleon-like powers. In its first exposition, as we have seen, it was based primarily on the undesirability of over-industrialization. But in this form it is not at all easy to reconcile with another eagerly advocated National Socialist ideal: the ideal of the 'Great Economy Space'. This concept was the forerunner of the war-time slogan of the 'New European Order'. What it amounted to was that Germany was to be the industrial and financial centre of a large block of vassal States, from Scandinavia to the Black Sea. These would be under her economic domination, and their economic systems would be organized to fit in with her requirements; in other words, they would on the one hand supply her with the raw materials and agricultural produce which she needed and on the other hand would offer a sure and stable market for her manufactured goods. Again, we are not concerned with the merits of this scheme as such, nor with the likelihood of its appealing to the other European countries concerned. But it entailed that Germany herself would remain predominantly an industrial country, at least in the sense of not aiming at agricultural self-sufficiency. It was thus directly contrary in spirit and trend to the ideal outlined by Hitler in *Mein Kampf*.

But the propagandists, not worried by the inconsistency, took over the 'Great Economy Space' concept and fitted it to their living-space arguments; with the result that the whole doctrine appears in two divergent and mutually contradictory versions.

that the system of marriage loans, which was undoubtedly the most efficacious of the National Socialist measures for immediately increasing the birth-rate, was not introduced for that purpose at all, but simply as a means of withdrawing women from the labour market and so reducing unemployment.

In the version we have so far been examining *Germans* are to have the same amount of land per head as other peoples. They are to be spread out over a wider area of territory until their density of population falls from 135 per square kilometre to the world average of about 16 per square kilometre. That implies that if the additional land acquired is already populated the inhabitants must be expelled. Otherwise the increase in the area of Germany will have been accompanied by an increase in the population within her frontiers and the density of population will not have fallen, or at any rate not by the required amount. It might even rise—if the areas taken over were more densely populated than Germany. For instance, when Italy annexed Albania that action was warmly approved at the time by Hitler, who was prepared to regard Albania as coming within Italy's 'living space'. But if the test of living space is density of population, then the result of taking over Albania was to *reduce* the Italian living space. For Albania had a larger population per square kilometre than had the rest of Italy's territorial possessions, so its annexation *increased* the overall density of population in the Italian Empire as a whole.

It is on this point that we can clearly see the chasm between the two versions of the living-space doctrine which the propagandists so carefully tried to conceal. They pretended, so as to give a façade of reasonableness to their argument, that what they demanded was simply to apportion the world's surface fairly among its inhabitants. But that was not what they really wanted. The demand for a living space for Germany in eastern Europe— or for that matter in the tropics—was a demand for new areas of land which could be exploited *with their existing populations* for the benefit of Germany. It was a demand in fact for a 'Great Economic Space', or, better, for an 'Exploitation Space'.

In this naked form, however, the argument lost much of its seeming reasonableness. Not every German would accept without qualms the idea that Germany was entitled 'according to the laws of a Divine Will' to exploit other peoples in her own interest. So it was worth while for the propagandists to go on pretending that all they wanted was 'living space' for German peasants.

On the other hand, even the 'Great Economic Space' form of the argument could be made to look plausible if it were connected with the demand for 'Equality of Rights'. It then ran as follows. Germany is admittedly not the most densely populated country in the world. *But* every one of the countries with a higher density has in addition a colonial empire, from which it makes up for the deficiencies of its living space at home. Germany is alone among the Great Powers in having nothing but the motherland to rely on; she therefore demands more living space not merely for their economic advantages but also as part of her claim to equality of rights.

Let us examine the argument in this second form.

First we note that it tacitly or openly assumes a distinction between peoples who are entitled to exploit and peoples who must expect to be exploited. The claim for equality of rights is a claim that Germany shall be recognized as belonging to the former category. It is thus not at all a humanitarian argument; if Poland (for instance) were to advance similar claims to more living space—as a country with no colonies and a density of population well above the average (though not so high as Germany's)—the National Socialist reaction would probably be that it was absurd and an impertinence to regard Poland as being on all fours with the German master race.

Secondly, it is an argument which can be used *either* to justify German conquest or domination inside Europe *or* to justify a claim to colonies. The latter version was the more plausible-sounding since most Europeans do in fact regard negroes as in some sense inferior to white men, and since the possession of colonies by European countries is a recognized institution, whereas the exploitation of one European country by another is not. Nevertheless, the European version of the claim had to be pressed as well, since the National Socialists needed it to justify their military plans in the eyes of the German people. Moreover, it was with expansion in Europe that Hitler was primarily interested. The demand for colonies came later, as an afterthought, and was indeed wholly inconsistent with all his earlier views on the subject.[1]

[1] Here are a few quotations from *Mein Kampf*: 'We must not look for a solution of this question [viz. of Living Space] in the acquisition of colonies but exclusively in gaining a settlement area which extends the territory of the motherland itself' (p. 741). 'We finally put an end to the "colonies and commerce" policy of the pre-war years and go over to the "land and soil" policy of the future' (p. 742). 'The political will and testament of the German nation in its dealings abroad should and must always in reason run: "see to it that the strength of your people derives its foundation not in colonies but in the soil of the home country in Europe"' (p. 754). On p. 753 Hitler

So the living-space doctrine was used as a justification *both* of conquest inside Europe *and* of the claim for colonies overseas.

The first of these points has far-reaching and fundamental implications to which we shall come back later. It will be one of the witnesses in our final inquiry on the issue of war guilt. Here all we need do is to note the light it throws on the doctrine of encirclement. We saw that the question whether there was an encirclement policy against Germany on the part of her neighbours, and if so whether it justified Germany in going to war against them so as to break the ring, turned upon the justice of Germany's plans. We now know what, under the National Socialists, Germany's plans were: not merely a few frontier adjustments or the protection of German-speaking minorities, but a deliberate drive for a great new 'Exploitation Space'. Germany's neighbour States wanted to prevent the achievement of this goal. They did try to 'encircle' her—not, however, in the sense of organizing an offensive alliance with a programme of invasion and conquest, but only in the sense of constructing a *cordon sanitaire* round Germany as a Power which *had* a programme of invasion and conquest. Largely this policy was inspired by self-interest and self-protection; but considerations of justice also played their part, especially in the case of the countries not immediately threatened by the German programme. And our verdict on the encirclement issue turns precisely on this question. The living-space doctrine as applied to Europe entails that Germany has the *right* to overrun the territories of neighbouring countries and to hold their peoples in subjection for the sake of German national interests; it claims that any wars carried out in the process of conquest, or for the sake of defending and retaining the territories conquered, are 'just' wars. The outside world denies that, as it would deny a similar claim put forward by any other nation. Which is right?

6.

Now as to the claim for colonies. This was first formally announced by Hitler at the Nuremberg Party Rally in September 1935, though it had been the subject of less official comment

declares his conviction that in the years before 1914 Germany should have 'renounced its senseless colonies policy' and should have concentrated on a 'determined Europe policy, of acquiring continental territory'—namely, at the expense of Russia.

for at least a year previously. Thereafter it was repeated with mounting passion and acerbity until the outbreak of war, except for one moment of relaxation in 1938 when Hitler, wanting to persuade England to give way over the Sudetenland crisis, said to the British Prime Minister, as a kind of bait, that the colonial question 'is not a matter for war; there will be no mobilization about that'. In fact, of course, Hitler would certainly have been willing to go to war about the colonies, and many Germans would have been ready to believe that such a war was a 'just' one. It is important to see why.

The claim for colonies was based on two main theses: first that colonies represented a vital *economic* need for Germany; and, secondly, that as a Great Power she had a *right* to them. The first was the one on which the main overt stress was laid; the second was the real driving force behind the claim.

The economic advantages of colonial possessions were regularly and fantastically overstated by the propagandists. Before 1914, as we saw in Chapter II, the German colonies were of no economic importance whatever to the motherland and in fact all except one of them cost more in administration than they yielded in products—to say nothing of the expense of maintaining a large navy for their defence. Even in the middle thirties their exports ran to no more than 200 million marks a year; that is to say, they were less than 1½ per cent. of Germany's total imports in 1928 and still only between 4 and 5 per cent. of Germany's greatly restricted imports during the immediate pre-war years.

Moreover, the return of her former colonies to Germany would not of itself have meant a net gain to her of even that amount. For throughout the twenties and thirties a large proportion of the trade of at least some of them was conducted with Germany. The outstanding example was that of the Cameroons, which was administered by a British mandate. Of the 281 Europeans living there in 1937, 176 were Germans, the remainder consisting almost entirely of government officials and missionaries. Of the total exports in that year four-fifths went to Germany—a larger quantity in absolute terms than during the years when the Cameroons were part of the German Colonial Empire.

And what about imports? The propagandists claimed that as the legal currency of the territory was sterling, not marks,

Germany was at a disadvantage in selling to the country as well as in buying from it. In so far as any disadvantage did accrue from this source it was due (as we saw in the last chapter) to Germany's own decision to maintain foreign exchange restrictions instead of allowing free exchange between the mark and other currencies. But in the case of the Cameroons there was no such disadvantage. For the plantation companies were allowed to pay their employees in marks and the latter could only, of course, be spent on German products. Moreover, the machinery and other equipment of the plantation operations was all German. With the result that Germany supplied the Cameroons in 1937 with 47.7 per cent—all but a half—of its total imports. And it is worth adding that in the view of the head of the Reich Colonial League, General Ritter von Epp, a share of that size represents what can reasonably be expected by the motherland of a colonial area. 'Germany', he said, 'must have again the natural predominance in exports and imports which falls everywhere to the State having the sovereignty over the territory. France's share in the imports of Morocco, for example, amounts to 43·7 per cent, Great Britain's share in the imports of Nigeria to 55·2 per cent, Belgium's share in the imports of the Congo to 43·4 per cent.'[1] Germany's share in the imports of the Cameroons does not show up badly in comparison with these figures.

The position with respect to the other mandated territories was admittedly not so favourable as this from the German point of view. But Germany was not frozen out from any of them (except from those administered by Japan), and she could have taken a much greater share in their trade than she in fact did if the National Socialists had decided to pursue the path of normal international trade instead of working for autarky behind a barbed-wire fence of currency restrictions.

But that, of course, does not end the matter. For the propagandists could still maintain that if the colonies were under German control they would be able enormously to increase their productivity and economic importance. According to General Ritter von Epp, the exports of the former German colonies could under National Socialist leadership be trebled within ten years. Even this figure—and it is certainly not an underestimate—is not very impressive. Assuming that all the

[1] *Zeitschrift für Politik*, Jan.-Feb. 1939, p. 35.

exports now went to Germany, they would still amount to less than 5 per cent. of Germany's total imports in 1928, and about 13 per cent. of total imports during the thirties. Moreover, in a detailed German study of the composition of these imports it emerges clearly that for the most part the materials to be obtained would have done little to change Germany's dependence on the outside world. In the matter of foodstuffs the colonies could make Germany more or less self-sufficient in respect of cocoa and bananas; they could supply a half of her demand for industrial gold, a quarter of her lead imports, a seventh of her copper imports, an eighth of her tin imports. None of this is of *major* importance, especially when it is remembered, first, that these figures only represent what the National Socialists claimed *might* be achieved after about ten years,[1] and secondly, that in a world war they would at once cease to be available to Germany owing to the effects of the blockade.

There is, however, one exception in all this. The propagandists claimed that the exploitation of the iron-ore fields of Togoland would make Germany largely independent of iron imports from the outside world.[2] We need not discuss the truth of this claim, nor the advantage to Germany in cutting loose from the iron mines of northern Sweden, practically on her own doorstep. But the achievement of this end would certainly have required the labour of tens of thousands of men as miners, smelters, transport workers, and so on. It was not intended that this labour should be sent out to Togoland from Germany itself, for all the complaints of over-population in the Reich. The work would have had to be done by the natives; and since there were not enough of them in Togoland itself, a new kind of slave traffic would have developed, thousands of natives being compulsorily transferred to Togoland from Germany's other African colonies. Nor is it to be supposed that the German masters of these natives would be more considerate for their welfare than they were of the Czech workers whom they forced to migrate to the Reich after the occupation of Prague. Even in pre-war days the German colonial administration, even if it was not as utterly brutal as sometimes alleged, was notorious for neglecting the health and welfare of the native

---

[1] See Pasemann, in *Zeitschrift für Politik*, Jan.-Feb. 1939, pp. 150 ff.
[2] Ibid.

populations; the National Socialists, with their racial theories, would not, one imagines, have been markedly more considerate.

And here we come upon a vital point, one which the propagandists systematically misrepresented. Throughout their whole campaign for the return of the colonies—throughout the whole of their campaign for a larger living space—they took it for granted that the only interests to be considered were those of the colonizing Power. And when Great Britain claimed to be thinking also of the well-being of the native population, the propagandists retorted with fantastic stories of British atrocities in Africa, in India, in fact throughout the whole of the British Empire.

Now nobody can deny that the past record of Britain in her treatment of the colonial peoples under her rule contains some black episodes. Nor is it to be disputed that even at the present day there are still colonial areas in which British practice is far short of British ideals. But the point is: Britain is aware of its responsibilities in this matter, there is a vigilant public opinion on the watch to expose and denounce any cases of shortcoming, and the result has been a steady and marked improvement right through the last forty years—an improvement which the war was not allowed to interrupt, and which will continue at an accelerated pace now that the war is over. We are here faced, once again, with the fundamental inability of the National Socialists to understand the workings of a democratic country. In Britain, as also in the United States, it often happens that statesmen and political parties express their belief in high ideals which are not fully reflected in their country's day-to-day policy. But that does not mean that the enunciation of the ideals is mere hypocrisy. For they represent goals for which the Government is working and towards the realization of which it can be and often is most vigorously pressed by public opinion; with the result that gradually—far too gradually for the liking of many—practice conforms to theory and the country's policy catches up on the ideal it has set itself.

So the belief in Great Britain that colonial government is first and foremost a question of looking after the interests of the native populations is a factor of front-rank importance for British colonial policy. And when the propagandists based their claim for colonies on the right to exploit these populations in the national interests of Germany, they merely made it that much less likely that Britain would acknowledge their right or meet their demands. As we saw in the last chapter, there was during the middle thirties a growing willingness to meet Germany on the colonial issue. The trend was at once reversed when the annexation of Austria, and the means used for bringing it about, began to open Englishmen's eyes to the sort of people the National Socialists really were.

I am not saying that Great Britain derives no economic advantages from her colonial possessions—though I must add that the advantage has been far less than the National Socialists regularly pretended and is accompanied by a sense of responsibility for the interests of the natives which the National Socialists conspicuously lacked. My own personal conviction, and it is shared by a growing number of people in Great Britain and by perhaps a majority in the United States, is that the colonial issue will never be finally settled until all colonial territories have either reached a stage of development in which they can become self-governing States in their own right, or are placed under some form of international control which regards safeguarding the interests of the native populations as the first obligation and the availability of the colony's natural resources to the whole outside world on equal terms as the second. Nor is there in principle any objection to my mind in *every* country's taking part in that control, so long as it accepts those two principles and seeks to have them realized. But when a country regards colonies simply as areas of exploitation—as a part of its own 'living space'—to be used exclusively to its own advantage; when it regards peoples of foreign race as by definition inferior to itself and claims that its own interest overrides their most elementary rights; then along with millions of people not merely in England but throughout the world, I say, no, that is not good enough. The record of the existing Powers may not be stainless, but at least it is better than the record of the National Socialists would have been if they had had colonies to administer; at least it recognizes what I want as an ideal to be worked for, at least it has shown signs of improvement in the past and bears promise of still greater improvement in the future.

By this time, it will be seen, we have moved far outside the purely economic sphere. That is as it should be. For, as was said at the beginning of this discussion, it is not in the economic sphere that the real gravamen of the German complaint about colonies rests. Even if it could have been demonstrated to a National Socialist that the acquisition of colonies would make no economic difference to Germany, even if the situation in the Cameroons had been repeated in all the former German colonies and for that matter in the colonized areas of the world as a whole, even if Germany had been given facilities to exploit the natural and human resources of the colonies to her heart's content—even then the National Socialists would not have been satisfied. There would have remained the question of prestige. So long as Britain and France had colonies and Germany had none they would have gone on feeling that Germany was being slighted, was not being accorded the full recognition of her status as a Great Power. This attitude to the colonies is reflected in the phrases used so frequently by the advocates of a 'colonies' policy: phrases about Germany's right to share in the 'cultural mission' of colonial administration, about her demanding to do her part in spreading European civilization among primitive peoples, and so on. If such language could be taken at its face value it would be worthy of respect. But neither the policy of Germany towards her colonies in the years before the First World War nor—still less—the attitude of the National Socialists to colonial questions gives the slightest support to any such picture. Germany wanted colonies during the twenties and thirties, partly indeed (as we have seen) because of the economic gains they might by ruthless exploitation yield her, but chiefly because she felt the deprivation of her colonies to be a humiliation—a sign that she was regarded as an outcast among the nations, unworthy of the privileges and responsibilities of a Great Power.

And that is the clue, is it not, to the strength of the whole 'Equality of Rights' argument as a means of persuading the German people to support National Socialist policy? It was, of course, useful to the propagandists when they were able to point to specific examples of economic or other loss as a basis on which to justify their claims. But the fundamental appeal was: The rest of the world regards Germany as inferior; give us your support and we will show them that they are wrong!

By the middle thirties the colonial issue was the only one on which Germany had not recovered full equality of rights. In

all other directions the Western Powers had granted her everything she asked for in this regard; had allowed her such a degree
of equality of rights as fatally to menace their own security.
Had they understood the real driving force behind the demand
for equal rights they would have acted differently, to the
infinite benefit of themselves, Germany, and the whole world.
They would have prevented rearmament, would have prohibited the reintroduction of conscription, would have resisted
the reoccupation of the Rhineland. To all of these they consented in the name of equality of rights. But that was not
enough for National Socialist Germany, nor would the return
of the colonies have made any material difference.

For the *fundamental* source of the German fear of being
thought inferior did not lie in any provisions of the Peace
Treaty, or indeed in any part of the policy of the Western
Powers. It lay in the fact that in the First World War Germany
had been beaten. And to the National Socialists, themselves
filled with resentment at past defeat and knowing that this
feeling was shared, if less intensely, by the great majority of
their fellow countrymen, there seemed only one way of wiping
out the humiliation: the reversal of the decision of the First
World War by a second in which Germany would be victorious;
or at least the establishment of Germany in a dominant military
position in Europe, if not in the world as a whole.

Therein lies the significance of the propaganda line which
became so common in German broadcasts and press articles
after the fighting had started; the line that the Second World War
was merely the last stage of an immense 'Thirty Years War',
which had started in August 1914. On January 30, 1942, Hitler
announced that for him the First World War had never come to
an end, and the theme was taken up by his followers with
enthusiasm. It made nonsense of the whole propaganda case for
Germany's peaceful intentions during the period between the
wars. It was an open and defiant declaration that Germany
had not accepted the military decision of 1918, that she regarded
the post-Versailles years as simply a breathing space, that she
was determined to reopen the struggle by force of arms at
whatever moment was most convenient to her. That the ordinary German citizen did not wholeheartedly share this view is
certain. But for him too it had its appeal. It enabled him to tell
himself that after all the armistice of 1918 did not represent

'defeat', but was merely the end of the first round in a fight in which the final verdict was yet to come. Had he been consistent he would not also and at the same time have held that in the Second World War Germany was the innocent victim of an unprovoked and criminal international conspiracy. But logical arguing was of little importance to ordinary Germans after Hitler had come to power, and of no importance at all after the outbreak of hostilities. Their overriding need was to be given self-confidence and an assurance of the justice of their cause, and *all* arguments were welcome which could meet that need, whether or not they were plausible in themselves or consistent with one another.

7.

Before we proceed to our final summing up on the question of responsibility for the war, let us briefly deal with one last argument used by the propagandists to convince the German people of the rightness of their cause; the argument, namely, that the war must be a just one and a war of self-defence because Hitler had made peace offer after peace offer, had suggested disarmament pacts, and friendly settlements of all outstanding questions—and his advances had all been contemptuously rejected; so that war was the only way out.

There are here three questions. First, *did* Hitler in fact make any peace offers? Secondly, did his opponents reject them, and if so why? And thirdly, what was the significance of such offers from his point of view?

The first question is simply answered. Peace offers in the strict sense could not, of course, be made until the war had already broken out. But in the wider sense of assurances of friendship, renunciations of aggressive plans, guarantees of the territorial integrity of other States and so on they were a regular part of Hitler's technique right through the first six and a half years of his régime. In the last chapter we had occasion to enumerate the more important of these conciliatory gestures. To them we need only add the two 'peace offers' contained in public speeches on October 6, 1939, and July 19, 1940—that is to say, after the end of the Polish and French campaigns. Both of them amounted to saying that as Germany had now achieved her immediate aim she was prepared to stop fighting.

The attitude of the Western Powers to the pre-war offers

of friendship was described in detail in the last chapter. At first they welcomed them eagerly, accepted Hitler's word, entered into agreements with him, allowed him to have his way in matters in which they had the legal right, as well as the power, to stop him. Not until the spring of 1939 were they finally convinced of his real objects. Then, indeed, their attitude changed. As we saw at the beginning of this chapter, Great Britain *did* contemptuously reject the 'guarantee of the continuance of the British Empire' which Hitler on August 29 volunteered to provide. And Great Britain also rejected, not less decisively and derisively, the 'offers' of October 1939 and July 1940. Her reasons were two. First, the offers contained no concessions of any sort on the questions at issue; the proposition put forward in each case was that if Britain would now agree in full with Germany's demands Germany would not punish her for having dared unsuccessfully to oppose them; in other words, they represented a call to Britain to admit defeat, and Britain did not recognize that she was defeated. Secondly, Britain knew by that time very well that whatever agreement Hitler made he would also break as soon as it suited his convenience; as soon as he was ready for his next coup. It was just not worth while thinking of entering into agreements with Hitler, even if he had been prepared (as he was not) to offer terms which Britain could have regarded as doing justice to her European Allies.

And that brings us to the third point. Some Germans may at the time have thought that *these* peace offers at least were sincerely meant; that if Britain had only given way over the Polish question Hitler would *really* have achieved all he wanted, the series of coups would have come to an end, and the world could have settled down to an enduring peace. If that was so, then, though Britain could even then not have been blamed for being sceptical in view of Hitler's previous record in the matter of keeping his word, yet Germany might also feel that in starting the fight in September, as in carrying it on during the following winter and in the summer of 1940, she was doing something to which she had been forced by the obstinacy and lack of faith of her opponents. But it was not so. Goebbels himself admitted as much with complete candour over a year later. 'No one imagines', he said, 'that the problems of Europe would have been finally solved if England and France had

accepted the peace offer made by the Fuehrer after the victorious
conclusion of the Polish campaign. We should have had to
fight again in a few years.'[1] A moment's thought will show that
in the light of this statement, by a man who after all knew
the facts about National Socialist policy, Britain was fully
justified in her scepticism. In October 1939 Hitler had set out
a list of terms on which (he said) an enduring peace might be
built. In November 1941 Goebbels declared that if those terms
had been accepted there would still have had to be war. In
other words, Hitler's 1939 terms were *not* his last demands;
he had still others up his sleeve which he would have produced
at the convenient moment and for the realization of which he
would have been ready to make war.

The peace offers of October 1939 and July 1940 were thus
as spurious as all Hitler's other agreements and promises.
Whether Hitler hoped that they would deceive Britain I do not
know; I suspect that he did, for he had an unbounded faith in
his own powers of convincing people of what he wanted them
to believe. Failing that, he could at least hope that *some* people
in the enemy countries would take him seriously; the offers
would thus create dissensions in the enemy camp. But the main
object of these offers was undoubtedly to impress public opinion
inside Germany itself—to make the ordinary German feel that,
since his leaders clearly did want peace, the fact that the war
was still continuing could not be the fault of Germany.

It is perhaps worth while drawing attention in this connexion
to an episode in the First World War. At the end of 1916 the
Governments of the Central Powers, at the initiative of Germany, made a 'peace offer' to the Allies. It contained no
specific terms—merely a promise that proposals would be put
forward at the Conference Table 'designed to assure national
existence, honour, and free scope for their peoples' and representing, 'they are convinced, an adequate basis for an enduring
peace'. The Central Powers added a warning of the consequences if the offer was not accepted. Germany and her allies,
they said, would then carry on the struggle ruthlessly and to
a victorious conclusion. *But*, they concluded, in that case
'they solemnly disclaim all responsibility before the bar of
world opinion and history'.

The technique, it will be observed, was exactly the same as

[1] See his article in *Das Reich*, November 9, 1941.

that employed twenty-three years later by Hitler. No enemy could conceivably have accepted this offer unless he were on the point of collapse—and the Allies were far from that in December 1916. But the offer might cause some heart-burning in the enemy camp and its rejection would certainly stiffen public opinion in Germany itself—as well as providing an excuse for introducing unrestricted U-boat warfare. Its spuriousness was finally shown up over a year later when the President of the Pan-German Association, Justizrat Klass, said: 'We can thank God on bended knees that the enemy did not accept our peace offer of December 12th, 1916'. By that time Germany was flushed with her successes in the east: she no longer needed to pretend that she was interested merely in 'national existence, honour, and free scope for her people'. She wanted more than that—annexation, exploitation space, European, perhaps world domination.

And in similar circumstances, towards the end of 1941, when he thought Russia was once more at the mercy of Germany, Hitler used almost the very words of Klass to express the same meaning. 'It was Providence, Almighty Providence, which prevented my peace offer from being accepted.'

Thus the same technique was used by Germany in two wars —or should one say in the two parts of the same war. In neither case did it deceive anybody; except perhaps the German people.

VII

WILL THERE BE A THIRD WORLD WAR?

W E are now at last ready for the final challenge on the issue of war guilt.

Let us first collect together the data yielded by earlier chapters.

(1) The Second World War was not from Germany's point of view a war of self-defence. For she was neither threatened with attack or invasion by any neighbour, nor were those of German blood outside her frontiers subject to any disabilities or sufferings that could not have been dealt with by peaceful negotiations.

(2) The war was from Germany's point of view only a 'just' war if 'justice' required that Germany should have the right to rule over and exploit neighbouring territories as part of her living space. If Germany had that right, then her opponents in organizing resistance to her in the interests of their own self-defence were guilty of 'injustice'—though even then not of aggression. The National Socialists held that Germany did have that right, thanks to their racial theories and their belief in the principle of right by conquest; Germany's opponents did not accept this view.

(3) Germany was not fighting for equality of rights, since apart from the colonial issue, which was not the occasion of the war, all the disabilities under which the Treaty of Versailles had placed her had been eliminated.

(4) The Western Powers had not shown themselves unwilling to meet Germany's demands; on the contrary they had given way on more than one occasion—and notably at Munich in September 1938, when doing so went directly contrary to what they felt to be reasonable and just—in the vain hope of preserving peace.

(5) The 'peace offers' with which Germany sought to shift responsibility for the war on to the shoulders of her opponents were neither genuinely meant nor were they such as any opponent could accept who believed in the justice of his cause and was not yet beaten.

(6) By his systematic use of treaties and agreements as strategical devices, to be broken and disregarded as soon as it

suited his convenience, Hitler had destroyed the value of a German pledge. Even if he had offered a promise which he sincerely meant to keep, with no unexpressed reservations about his right to change his mind later, the outside world would not have trusted it, and could not have been expected to trust it, in view of his past record.

(7) Ever since Germany's defeat in the First World War influential groups, including the leaders of the Army and of heavy industry, had been at work preparing, by secret rearmament and propaganda among the German people, for a renewal of the struggle. Hitler was put into power by their efforts and as their agent. Hitler himself, both before and subsequently, made it clear that he shared their point of view. For him, as for them, the war of 1914 had never come to an end.

(8) Ever since Germany's defeat in the First World War these same groups spread about propaganda to the effect that Germany had not really been beaten and that the Treaty of Versailles represented an unbearably unjust and oppressive peace. Neither of these contentions had any foundation in fact, but they were generally believed in Germany because the German people wanted to believe them. It was ready to accept uncritically any account of the end of the last war which would save it from what it felt to be an unbearable humiliation— namely the fact that it had been defeated.

That is the evidence provided by our investigations. The question that it raises in the mind of any outside observer is, not whether Hitler's Germany was responsible for the Second World War, but why anybody who supported Hitler and accepted his doctrines should be concerned about the question of war responsibility at all. We shall come back to that question in a moment. Let us first give our verdict on the facts.

It is not certain, though highly likely, that Germany 'fired the first shot'. The question, however, is not as such important, since the justification for 'firing the first shot' depends on the military circumstances leading up to it.[1]

Germany was not the first to 'declare war'. In fact under Hitler Germany never 'declared' war until the end of 1941, when she did so on the United States. This is also wholly unimportant, however, since the question at issue is one of deeds, not

[1] See above, pp. 131 f.

words. In 1914 it was Germany who declared war on both
France and Russia—but nobody, least of all the propagandists,
has regarded that as being in itself proof of Germany's responsibility for the First World War.

On the other hand, Germany certainly *started* the war. The
death of the peace came when Hitler gave the order to the
German army to invade Poland on September 1, 1939.

Germany was also *responsible* for the war in the correct sense
of that word. For from her point of view the war was *not* one of
self-defence, whatever the propagandists may have pretended;
and it is only when one is fighting in self-defence—namely
against an imminent threat of attack from outside—that one can
claim that one is not 'responsible' for a war which one has oneself started.

This is a point of vital importance for clear thinking. The
last chapter has shown us that the propagandists' case on the
subject throughout depended not on the claim that the war was
one of self-defence, but that it was a war of justice, as they
interpreted that concept. The arguments which tended to
suggest that it was also a war of self-defence were, we saw, an
empty camouflage. Now if Germany's case was that her war
aims were in themselves just and reasonable, then why should
she shrink from admitting 'responsibility' for the war? The
logical line would surely be to accept and even glory in that
responsibility, on the ground that it was a responsibility undertaken in the cause of justice and the right. Being 'responsible'
for something only implies guilt if the thing in question is as
such clearly bad. On the other hand, it is a recognized and
indeed almost universal phenomenon that those who have a bad
conscience about something they have done will try to escape
the sense of *guilt* by denying *responsibility*. And that is why the
propagandists laid so much stress on showing that the Second
World War, when it came, would be a war, not merely of justice,
but of self-defence. They hoped to reassure any German who
might remain unconvinced on the justice question; he was to tell
himself that Germany *could* not have been 'guilty' of having
caused the Second World War because she was not responsible
for its outbreak at all

But with the collapse of any suggestion that the war was
started by Germany in self-defence, that way out is barred.
Germany's 'responsibility' for the war is clear: the question is

whether and to what extent that responsibility involved her in 'guilt'.

Again, however, we must ask why that question matters. The National Socialists were people who believed that might is right and that in all international issues the only thing that matters is who is the stronger. I need not waste time citing evidence on this point. It was made clear by the propagandists a countless number of times that in their view the question of justice and morals just did not arise in connexion with Germany's attitude to foreign countries. They were to be regarded as 'natural enemies'; against the interests of Germany they had no rights whatever; if Germany needed their territory as part of her living space, and their populations as her slaves, she was fully entitled to attack and conquer them. Views of this sort were, I say, repeated over and over again by the National Socialists. It was therefore utterly inconsistent on Hitler's part to be *also* concerned whether the outer world would or would not admit that Germany's claims were 'justified'—unless of course his talk about the justice of Germany's claims was simply and solely a device for securing support at home and dulling fears and suspicions abroad. I do not believe this, however; I am convinced that Hitler, in spite of all his war preparations and plans, in spite of his contempt for the idea of keeping his own promises, in spite of his glorification of war as the supreme expression of human nobility and as the medium in which the German people would prove its worth, was nevertheless genuinely conscious, at least in some moods, of the importance of the concepts of justice and fair dealing even as between nation and nation. And certainly most Germans were touched by a respect for that ideal—whether for its own sake or merely because they realized that other peoples believed in it and wanted to rehabilitate themselves in those peoples' eyes.

But it is no use attempting to believe in justice and in rule by force at one and the same time. Germany, let us presume—that is to say the German people—really wanted to settle down in peace and harmony with the rest of the world. But she did not draw the logical consequences from that desire. For she also wanted to assert herself by force and armed might. By following that latter desire she laid *upon herself* the burden of guilt for the Second World War. It is there because she was not true to an ideal in which she herself believed.

And that is why the ingenuities and tortuousnesses of the propagandists were never able wholly to set the mind of the ordinary German at rest. For he was always fundamentally in his heart aware (I believe) of an incompatibility among his own ideals and was always frightened of the dilemma with which that incompatibility confronted him. The dilemma can be presented as follows. Do you or do you not accept the thesis that the national interests of Germany entitle her to trample on the rights of Poles and of other peoples whom she alleges to be an inferior order of human beings? If you do, then why did you worry about the 'justice' of your cause in the Second World War? If you do not, if you admit that Poles and Czechs and Russians—yes, and Jews too—have their rights, even against Germans, then you were guilty of a sin against your own principles when you supported a policy which ignored and trampled on those principles. Your accusers are not only the peoples against whom you have fought and by whom you have for the second time been beaten. Your accusers are also your own ideals, the ideals to which you know you have not been true.

Nor is this conclusion affected by arguments which attempt to draw a distinction between the National Socialists and the mass of the German people; on the contrary, it is strengthened by such arguments. Let us grant that it was the National Socialists who were *responsible* for the war. They prepared for it, worked for it, precipitated it, for their own ends and in terms of their own philosophy of force. From their point of view the German people was simply one of the factors in the situation. It had to be brought on to their side and made to do what they wanted. The methods they adopted to achieve this have been described already: terror, habituation to war-time conditions, propaganda. And the most effective of these was propaganda. The whole of this book has been concerned with showing how overwhelming was the victory of the propagandists over the German people, which allowed itself to be worked up into a frenzied and fanatical belief in their distortions of history. They could never have gained such a victory if those whom they were addressing had not been willing victims; had not *wanted* to be convinced. *In that sense* the vast majority of Germans were themselves National Socialists. Even when they were not members of the Party, even if they denied all interest in and understanding of political matters or felt themselves to be out of sympathy with

the methods and point of view of their leaders, yet they subscribed to the National Socialists' demand for a strong and
aggressive Germany, backed them in their war effort, felt pride
in their successes. Terror was only needed against the few, and
against some of these, a brave and honoured minority, even
terror was powerless. The majority responded to propaganda
and identified themselves with the National Socialist cause.
Only after the war had started did they begin to shrink back,
feeling no great joy in Germany's initial triumphs; becoming
worried at the brutality of German behaviour in the occupied
territories; longing above all for peace and friendship with the
other Great Powers. But by then it was too late; the chains
with which they had allowed themselves to be fettered were not
to be thrown off. So they relapsed into resignation, either
accepting the propagandists' lies about what would happen to
them in case of defeat or consoling themselves with the argument that they were helpless to prevent matters from taking
their course.

If that is at all an accurate picture of the attitude of the
German people to the National Socialists during the past eleven
and a half years, then the conclusion must be that it had a minor
share in the *responsibility* for the war and a major share in the
war *guilt*. Its responsibility was that it lent itself as a willing tool
in the hands of the National Socialist war-makers; its guilt was
that it did so in defiance of principles of justice and ethics to
which it in its heart subscribed.

This is not of course a legal question. Those who have committed crimes can be dealt with in courts of law and, if their
guilt is proved, can be punished; and the United Nations have
declared their determination that Germans who are accused of
war crimes will be brought to trial. The guilt of which I
am speaking cannot be proved or disproved by a legal tri-
bunal. It is a matter which only the individual concerned can
settle, and there can be no question of punishment from outside,
except in so far as the events of the war and its result are con-
strued by him in that light. When France was defeated in 1940
one of the immediate results was the growth of a feeling—expressed most clearly in the early speeches of Pétain—that her
sufferings and humiliations were a judgement on her for past
sins and that she must undergo a process of spiritual purification
before being able to look the world proudly in the face again.

Perhaps a similar feeling will emerge in Germany: perhaps, on the contrary, a large number of Germans will be able to say to themselves that they were never untrue to their ideals, that they did what they could, that no guilt rests upon them. In either case what matters here is their own feelings about themselves, not what the outside world thinks or believes. It is of secondary importance whether *I* think you guilty (in the sense of the word here under discussion) if *you* are genuinely certain that you are not. And an excessive desire to be thought well of and liked by other people is merely a sign of internal unsureness.

But the real test on this whole issue will come during the next few years. It is quite certain that many thousands in Germany are to-day once again, as were their predecessors in 1919, asking themselves how to restore Germany's military strength—how to embark her once again on the path of conquest and aggression. For them the war which started in 1914 has even now not come to an end: and as twenty-five years ago, so now they will set out to reawaken nationalist ambitions among their fellow-countrymen. There will be a new version of the stab-in-the-back legend; that is quite certain. At the moment I do not know what form it will take; but *somehow*, in *some* form, the story will be spread about that the German Army was not *really* 'defeated' but succumbed to treachery. Again, life in Germany will be very hard for years to come and the terms of the peace will undoubtedly be severe—and it will be insisted that they are for that reason not merely humiliating, but also 'unjust'. The fact that Germany by all appearances came so near to final victory in the summer of 1940 and again in the late autumn of 1941 will be used to show that in a Third World War she might at last achieve the goal. In these and other ways the propagandists will be at work, trying, doggedly and skilfully, to keep alive the spirit of war and conquest. And the question is: Will the German people once again swallow the bait?

From the point of view of the world as a whole this is not a question of over-riding importance. The United Nations have learned from the history of the last twenty-five years. They made many mistakes during the interval between the two world wars, as we have had occasion to notice more than once in the course of this book; mistakes due to ignorance, to laziness, to national selfishness. They too failed to live up to their own ideals, and must accept a measure of guilt not, indeed, for the Second World War, for which they had no responsibility, but for the missed opportunities of the peace. They will try to do better this time; and though in many directions they will doubtless fall short of full success, for the war has left a legacy of bitterness which may well at times cloud their judgement, yet in one respect they will certainly stand firm—they will see to it that even if Germany has the will she will not have the power to precipitate a Third World War. This time there will be no secret rearmament, no training of German airmen on Russian flying-fields, no re-forming of cadres for a new German Army. Even if the propagandists were to achieve a second triumph over the minds and wills of the German people, as complete as their triumph in the days of National Socialism, there will still be no Third World War; the United Nations will see to that.

But for Germany itself the success or failure of the propagandists will be a matter of crucial moment; for it will determine whether the German people must for an indefinite period be treated as an enemy people, disliked, suspected, if necessary held down by physical force; or whether as the years pass and the harsh memories of the war begin to fade it gradually becomes accepted as a friend and ally against all disturbers of the peace.

The danger is a real one. As we saw in an earlier chapter, much of the success of German propaganda to the outside world during the twenties was due to the work not of professional propagandists but of ordinary Germans who, when they travelled abroad or met Englishmen or Americans in Germany, passed on with passionate sincerity the propaganda they had themselves absorbed and were the more efficient in disseminating lies the more they were themselves convinced that these lies were the truth. If the propagandists have their way the same process will be started again after this war. Already we can see its beginnings. Since the summer of 1943 there have been many Germans in Great Britain and America—including people of all types, from genuine refugees from National Socialist oppression to aggressive German prisoners of war—who have seized every opportunity to impress upon anybody they met that the United Nations would do well to treat Germany 'more fairly' than the Allies did in 1919, if they want to avoid yet a third world war. Such arguments will not make any difference to the terms of the peace settlement. They will not convince those against whom they are addressed. But they are capable of affecting decisively, and for a long time to come, the attitude of the outside world to Germany—the willingness of people of other nations to believe in the sincerity of Germany's desire for a lasting peace.

This book has been written in the belief that, by studying what the National Socialists said and did in the past, one can forearm oneself against what their successors will say and do, subterraneously, in the future. Ever since the foundation of the Reich Germany has been the storm centre of Europe; she has been the protagonist of militarism and of right by conquest, she has worked for European, at times for world, domination. But in some of the earlier wars there may be room for argument; her apologists could point to evidence that the responsibility was not entirely hers. In the case of the Second World War the matter is beyond all question. No German who seriously considers the evidence I have presented to him here can have any doubt about it: under Hitler's leadership Germany stirred up trouble, fomented hatred and enmity among the peoples of the world, precipitated the disaster of the war. A large part of the blame rests with the German people itself for accepting and supporting such rulers. Only the German people can set matters right; if namely it approaches the coming years in a spirit of realistically accepting defeat, abandoning evil and useless dreams of renewing the struggle, and settling down to restore Germany's former greatness in the realms of peace and co-operation instead of war and strife.

The Text of the Fourteen Points and the Modifications introduced by the Allies

THE Fourteen Points as originally enunciated by President Wilson in a speech on January 8, 1918, ran as follows:

1. Open covenants of peace openly arrived at, after which there shall be no private international understandings of any kind, but diplomacy shall proceed always frankly and in the public view.

2. Absolute freedom of navigation upon the seas outside territorial waters alike in peace and in war, except as the seas may be closed in whole or in part by international action for the enforcement of international covenants.

3. The removal, so far as possible, of all economic barriers and the establishment of an equality of trade conditions among all the nations consenting to the peace and associating themselves for its maintenance.

4. Adequate guarantees given and taken that national armaments will be reduced to the lowest point consistent with domestic safety.

5. A free, open-minded, and absolutely impartial adjustment of all colonial claims, based upon a strict observance of the principle that in determining all such questions of sovereignty the interests of the populations concerned must have equal weight with the equitable claims of the Government whose title is to be determined.

6. The evacuation of all Russian territory, and such a settlement of all questions affecting Russia as will secure the best and freest co-operation of the other nations of the world in obtaining for her an unhampered and unembarrassed opportunity for the independent determination of her own political development and national policy, and assure her of a sincere welcome into the society of free nations under institutions of her own choosing and, more than a welcome, assistance also of every kind that she may need and may herself desire. The treatment accorded Russia by her sister nations in the months to come will be the acid test of their goodwill, of their comprehension of her needs as distinguished from their own interests, and of their intelligent and unselfish sympathy.

7. Belgium, the whole world will agree, must be evacuated and restored without any attempt to limit the sovereignty which she enjoys in common with all other free nations. No other single act will serve as this will serve to restore confidence among the nations in the laws which they have themselves set and determined for the government of their relations with one another. Without this healing

act the whole structure and validity of International Law is for ever impaired.

8. All French territory should be freed, and the invaded portions restored, and the wrong done to France by Prussia in 1871 in the matter of Alsace-Lorraine, which has unsettled the peace of the world for nearly fifty years, should be righted in order that peace may once more be made secure in the interest of all.

9. A readjustment of the frontiers of Italy should be effected along clearly recognizable lines of nationality.

10. The peoples of Austria-Hungary, whose place among the nations we wish to see safeguarded and assured, should be accorded the freest opportunity of autonomous development.

11. Rumania, Serbia, and Montenegro should be evacuated, occupied territories restored, Serbia accorded free and secure access to the sea, and the relations of the several Balkan States to one another determined by friendly counsel along historically established lines of allegiance and nationality, and international guarantees of the political and economic independence and territorial integrity of the several Balkan States should be entered into.

12. The Turkish portions of the present Ottoman Empire should be assured a secure sovereignty, but the other nationalities which are now under Turkish rule should be assured an undoubted security of life and an absolute unmolested opportunity of autonomous development, and the Dardanelles should be permanently opened as a free passage to the ships and commerce of all nations under international guarantees.

13. An independent Polish State should be erected which should include the territories inhabited by indisputably Polish populations, which should be assured a free and secure access to the sea, and whose political and economic independence and territorial integrity should be guaranteed by international covenant.

14. A general association of nations must be formed under specific covenants for the purpose of affording mutual guarantees of political independence and territorial integrity to great and small States alike.

When the Allies were invited by the President in October 1918 to express their assent to these points, they did so with the following three modifications:

(i) Point 2 was deleted as representing a controversial issue between Britain and America which could better be settled at a later stage.

(ii) A rider was added to Points 7 and 8 which ran: 'Compensation will be made by Germany for all damage done to the civilian population of the Allies and their property by the aggression of Germany by land, by sea and from the air.'

(iii) Point 9 was modified in view of the obligations already entered into by Britain and France towards Italy (in the Treaty of London of April 26, 1915) whereby Italy had been promised the Brenner frontier and the City and Hinterland of Trieste.

With these modifications the Fourteen Points represented the agreed view of the Allies as to the shape of the peace settlement.

INDEX

Abyssinia, 116.

Agadir crisis 1911, 58.

Albania, 154.

Allies in First World War: charges against by National Socialists, 1–2; failure to understand German attitude regarding end of the war, 3; March 1918 German offensive fails, 4–5; effect of counter-offensives, 5–6; decisive air superiority, 6 and *n.*; public opinion and German request for armistice, 12 ff.; unpreparedness for armistice, 13*n.*; plans for supplying foodstuffs to Germany after the Armistice, 30 ff.; and Treaty of Versailles, 37 ff.; effect on of treaties of Brest-Litovsk and Bucharest, 42; terms for armistice, 44 ff.; and Polish problem, 49; claims for security against Germany, 50; aware of German rearmament in 1920s, 83 ff.; post-war disunity among, 88.

Alsace-Lorraine, 46, 48, 50, 55, 93.

America. *See* United States.

Anti-Comintern Pact, 101.

Appeasement, 113.

Armistice 1918: German request for, 3 ff.; High Command continues to press for, 9; Ludendorff's tortuous behaviour, 8, 9 ff.; Wilson insists that conditions of armistice be left to Allied commanders, 8; Gröner states that armistice is only alternative to surrender, 9; German army saved from knock-out blow by armistice, 22; effect on revolution in Germany, 24–5; Armistice terms frustrated Ludendorff's hope of renewing hostilities, 29; ways in which terms were not severe enough, 29–30.

Atrocity propaganda by National Socialists, 141–2, 160.

Austria annexed by Hitler, 103–4, 111, 114, 125, 161.

Austria-Hungary, 4, 6, 35, 41, 46, 47 and *n.*, 54, 146–7.

Autarky in Germany, 59, 92 ff., 158.

Axis, formation of the, 101.

B.B.C. foreign news service, 117.

Belgium, 49, 61, 69, 106, 128, 150*n.*, 158.

Benes, Dr., 115, 116*n.*

Bismarck, Count Otto von, 58; reparations from France in 1871, 60.

'Black Militia', German, 78, 79.

Blockade of Germany: German allegation that it was unjustly maintained after the Armistice, 1; effect on Germany's war effort, 22; not the cause of German food-shortage after the Armistice, 36.

Blum, Leon, 123.

Bohemia annexed by Hitler, 105.

Bolshevism, 25, 26, 110, 111, 114, 119.

Brest-Litovsk, Treaty of, 23*n.*, 40 ff., 60–1, 117.

Britain, *passim*; abandons gold standard, 94–5; friendly to Germany in 1920s, 108 ff.; critical attitude towards Treaty of Versailles, 108 ff.; attitude towards National Socialists, 110 ff.; guarantee to Poland, 117 ff., 137. *See also* Imperial Preference.

Brussels Agreement, 33, 34.

Buch-Müller, Col., 82.

Bucharest, Treaty of, 23*n.*, 41–2.

Buelow, Prince von, 135.

Bulgaria, 4, 5.

Burian, Baron, 42.

Cameroons, 55, 157–8.

Chamberlain, Neville, 105, 107, 115, 116*n.*, 122, 157.

Churchill, Winston, 25.

Colonies, German, 50, 55 ff., 109, 111 ff., 155 and *n.*, 156 ff., 168.

Congo, 158.

Cossmann, Professor, 17, 18.

Czechoslovakia, 47*n.*, 104–5, 107, 114 ff., 125, 127, 129, 138, 139, 141, 142, 146.

Danzig, 49, 55, 105, 106*n.*, 116, 123, 124 ff., 140–1.

Dawes Plan, 73, 86*n.*, 87.

Denmark, 106. *And see* Schleswig.

Dibelius, Professor, 110.

Disarmament, 54–5, 68, 69.

Disarmament Commission, 52.

Economic crisis, 76, 85, 94.

Economic measures against Germany, 1–2.

Economic nationalism, 71 ff., 92 ff. *And see* Autarky.

Eden, Anthony, 114.

Edward VIII, 120.

Encirclement, doctrine of, 134 ff.